Christianity at the Cross-roads

by

George Tyrrell

author of "Lex Credendi," etc.

Third impression

Wipf & Stock
PUBLISHERS
Eugene, Oregon

Wipf and Stock Publishers
199 W 8th Ave, Suite 3
Eugene, OR 97401

Christianity at the Cross-Roads
By Tyrrell, George
ISBN: 1-59752-976-1
Publication date 9/21/2006
Previously published by Longmans, Green, and Co., 1910

CONTENTS

		PAGE
INTRODUCTION	. . . .	vii
PREFACE	. . . .	xv

PART I

CHRISTIANITY AND CATHOLICISM

I.	MODERNISM AND TRADITION	3
II.	VARIOUS FORMS OF MODERNISM . . .	6
III.	THE OLD ORTHODOXY	14
IV.	THE NEW ORTHODOXY	21
V.	NEWMAN'S THEORY OF DEVELOPMENT . .	29
VI.	FIRST RESULTS OF NEW TESTAMENT CRITICISM	35
VII.	THE CHRIST OF LIBERAL PROTESTANTISM .	39
VIII.	THE CHRIST OF ESCHATOLOGY . . .	46
IX.	THE CHRIST OF CATHOLICISM . . .	62
X.	THE ABIDING VALUE OF THE APOCALYPTIC IDEA	91
XI.	THE TRUTH-VALUE OF VISIONS . .	105

		PAGE
XII.	THE APOCALYPTIC VISION OF CHRIST	114
	a. THE TRANSCENDENCY OF THE KINGDOM	114
	b. IMMORTALITY	127
	c. RESURRECTION	138
	d. THE IMMEDIACY OF THE KINGDOM	157
	e. THE SON OF MAN	171
	f. GOD AND SATAN	191
	g. THE IDEA OF ATONEMENT	199
	h. THE PHENOMENAL AND THE SPIRITUAL	202
XIII.	THE APOCALYPTIC VISION AND THE CATHOLIC CHURCH	210

PART II
CHRISTIANITY AND RELIGION

I.	EXCLUSIVENESS AND INTOLERANCE	223
II.	THE UNIFICATION OF RELIGION	229
III.	THE SCIENCE OF RELIGIONS	245
IV.	CHARACTER OF AN UNIVERSAL RELIGION	252
V.	THE RELIGION AND PERSONALITY OF JESUS	261
VI.	THE CHURCH AND ITS FUTURE	274

INTRODUCTION

"WHEN the work is finished labour ceases, weary man enters into his rest." These words are in the book that lies before us, and the manuscript of that book lay open on his desk, and was receiving its last touches, when the worker was laid low, and the words were fulfilled. For some days, while the struggle between life and death was carried on in the little adjoining room, one did not even dream of moving the pages from where they rested. One thought at any moment to see him rise, as he had so often done after periods of pain and prostration, and go straight back to the unfinished task, as though to live and to work were, for him, but different names for the same thing. As long ago as November 11th, 1901, he said in a letter: "I am always hurried to get things in before death overtakes me, and am restless while anything is unfinished that I have once begun. Could I feel secure of a year . . . but I always think it may be in a week"; and this disposition never altered. It was as though his work were his fate; as though he were ever driven forward to the accomplishment of labours which were to bring to the labourer himself an ever new harvest of suffering and pain. For his work was not of the kind which reaps its reward in the satisfaction of ambition or the acquisition of fame. Such things were not classed by him among the realities of life. Peace of soul, undisturbed friendship, study and prayer, nature and books, and, last but not least, the altar from which he had been exiled, these would have been to him the realities and the true goods of life. But it was not to be. Almost as one unwilling, he was forced into combat; almost against his will, he remained in it to the last. With each book he seemed to hope that he might now steer his bark into stiller waters; might turn from the immediate and storm-stirring actualities to the quiet study of calm and universal problems; but each time he was disappointed, and had again to wield his pen in the more pressing cause. In this work his hopes came, I think, nearer to fulfilment than they had ever done before, and perhaps, had he lived, it would have been to the most fundamental questions of spiritual philosophy that he would henceforth have devoted himself. The book itself suggests this likelihood.

But, on the other hand, how are we to know? May not such an idea be as illusory as the hope, one had so deeply and constantly cherished, that his stormy day would close in a peaceful evening? that he would, before the end, find rest, even on this earth?

Anyhow, it was not to be, and he has entered into a peace more profound, and yet more living, than any which we could have planned for him.

That Father Tyrrell had any special consciousness of approaching death we have no reason to suppose; and yet, as though a certain sense of change were pressing on him, he has occupied himself, in this book as in no other, with the question of immortality; with an examination of the value of this life, a study of its relations to the next.

And his verdict is uncompromising. No ideal that is capable of realisation in this world is capable of appeasing the heart of man, whose hunger is for a transcendent kingdom, ruled by a transcendent God. Something more and something greater than all that life, under its present conditions, can offer; something after which we grope, without seeing it; something for which we long, without comprehending it; something which will explain us to ourselves as no human wisdom can explain us; this is what religion is to stand for, if it be religion at all, and not merely a scheme of philosophy, however enlightened. And this, too, is what Christ is to stand for, if He is to be the Christ of our religious aspirations; not the Christ of humanitarianism and philanthropy, but the Christ of a transcendent kingdom.

There are souls to whom the idea of God presents itself chiefly under its metaphysical and mystical aspect; there are others, of whom, I think, Father Tyrrell was one, who are eminently Christ-lovers and Christ-worshippers.

"The faith," he writes in this book, "in His own Christhood that Jesus, by the power of His personality, was able to plant in His Apostles, has been continually reinforced by the experience of those who have found Him, in effect, their Redeemer, the Lord and Master of their souls, their Hope, their Love, their Rest—in short, all that they mean by God."

To the lover of Christ the Christological problem is more painful and arduous than is the ecclesiastical problem to the lover of the Church. Father Tyrrell faced them both, and in this book we have his last—I will not say it was necessarily his final—treatment of the double problem. His answer was, as he believed, not likely to please any party—but parties matter little; it was to the single mind and soul and to humanity at large that, with a truly Catholic instinct, he ever addressed himself.

He deals first with the relation of Christ to the

Catholic Church; next with the relation of the religion of Christ to religion in general. He finds that the Catholic Church has, on the whole, preserved the message of Christ more faithfully than any other; and he believes that in Christianity is to be found the germ of that future universal religion for which we all look. The Church has fulfilled her end, because she has kept for us the Christ of the Gospels; not a modernised Christ, made up to meet the latest requirements, but the Christ who spoke in the categories of His place and time, while His message was for men of all places and all times. And in that message is the seed of future religion—a religion whose need is more and more pressingly apparent; a religion for which all humanity is crying, weary of petty divisions and disputes, yearning for a truth that shall be the possession of all. But it is not an entirely new religion that can fulfil this demand; the future must grow from the present as the present has grown from the past.

This is not the kind of apology to satisfy the majority of Catholics, who ask for blind, not open-eyed, adherence. But why should they read this work at all? Why should they not live on—as the writer himself would have urged them to do—in the peace of their own undisturbed convictions?

But for those Catholics who must love the Church in another way, or not at all, the book before us has a message of hope and consolation. For here is no faithfulness grounded on the habits of a spiritual home—the writer had learned to live homeless; nor is there a mere clinging to those sacramental graces which the Church can offer us—since of those graces he had been deprived; but here is faith in the Church as having guarded, amidst all her imperfections, the treasure committed to her by Jesus Christ.

A still further problem will suggest itself here to those who have faced anything of the perplexities of Gospel criticism, a problem which most certainly presented itself to the author of this book. He saw quite clearly that there are elements in the Gospel which seem to find their development in just those characteristics of ecclesiastical policy most repugnant to a more spiritual conception of religion and Christianity. His final answer to that difficulty he has not been able to give—but the book before us surely suggests, at least, the lines on which that answer might have been framed. No evasion of difficulties would ever have been his solution—of that one may at least be certain. He would have drained to the dregs that cup of bitter knowledge which truth so often offers us; he would have driven on, to their fullest conclusion, the hard premisses which study and research lay bare. But the mystic would not have been slain by the critic; the believer by the objector. Through the letter to the spirit; through the human to the divine; through the Church to Christ; through Christ to God; the way might have been perilous and terrible, but it would not have been forsaken for any easier path. And the victory would have been such as can only be gained by those who have shrunk from no hardship of the campaign.

NOTE

WE may take this work as having been, substantially, finished before the writer's death. But it had not been revised, and the second part even suggests the possibility of some further additions. Also, he had but partially indicated the divisions and titles of chapters. For any imperfections, therefore, in the execution of these details of form, the executor has to crave the indulgence of readers, while also thanking Mr. A. R. Waller for his kind help in the revision of proofs.

M. D. PETRE.

PREFACE

THE hope of a synthesis between the essentials of Christianity and the assured results of criticism is very widespread nowadays, and those who share it are commonly called Modernists or Liberals. There is a marked division of Modernists according as their tendency is to consider that alone to be essential to Christianity which agrees with their idea of the assured results of criticism, or to consider as the only assured results of criticism those that fit in with their conception of the essentials of Christianity. Both tendencies are vicious and, if unchecked, destroy the very idea of Modernism, which professes to consider each interest impartially, without respect to the other, in the belief and hope that the results will prove harmonious. Religion cannot be the criterion of scientific truth, nor science of religious truth. Each must be criticised by its own principles.

It is extremely hard for a Christian to look straight at his religion without regarding science out of the corner of his eye, or to face science without a similar side-glance at religion. But the effort must be made. In these pages I have asked myself frankly what I should consider the essence of Christianity were I not acquainted with the results of criticism; and how much of criticism I should admit if I cared nothing for Christianity. It does not seem to me that the results are very harmonious, but I should be sorry to say they were hopelessly irreconcilable. Indeed, the discord is much less than I had expected. To guard against bias I have inclined to the more extreme position on both sides. If I have overstated the difficulty so much the better.

But the purpose of these pages is in no wise to make an apology for Christianity and Catholicism; nor yet to defend Modernism from the attacks of its prejudiced enemies; nor to defend it at all; but rather to save it from its friends—from those amiable Liberal critics, who welcome it for precisely the same mistaken reason as those for which ultramontanism condemns it. It seems ungrateful and ungracious to criticise those who proffer sympathy where so little is to be had. Yet it is not quite honest to accept a gift intended for another address. So precious is praise that, if we do not deserve it, we are tempted to accept it with the intention of deserving it, and of becoming what we are supposed already to be. Every student of nature recognises the value of prepayments of merit. But he who would guard his liberty will be shy of incurring such debts of honour, and will decline what he knows to be unmerited praise. Would that all Modernists did so, and had declined to sacrifice the originality, distinction and solitude of their position to their desire for approbation; with the result of seeming to make much ado about nothing, and of arriving laboriously at a banal and facile solution, of which the world is well-nigh weary.

Between the Modernism of these, and that of *L'Évangile et l'Église*, there is scarcely a thought in common. Even if the illustrious author of that classical work has ceased to regard its position as practicable in view of the subsequent action of the Roman Church, that is no reason for giving its name to a precisely contrary position—to the Liberal Protestantism against which it was a protest. Hope is largely subjective, neither kindled nor killed by objective reasoning. If we have no hope in the Modernist position let us say so and adopt some other, or none at all, and cease to call ourselves by its name. Clear naming is essential to clear thinking; a spade is not a shovel.

If I find fault with some of the mistakenly sympathetic critics of Modernism, I admit that they are not without excuse, and that the blame lies partly with those Catholics who, simply because they are modern, call themselves Modernists. I own, however, to intense irritation in reading some of these well-meaning critiques. Their line of argument is almost stereotyped. They begin by dilating on the lethal stagnation and immobility of Rome. They then announce the astounding discovery of a little Goshen of enlightenment amid the waste of Egyptian darkness; of a group of Roman Catholics who, in spite of the Index and the vigilance of the terrible Inquisition, have dared to read and think for themselves, with the inevitable result of developing strong protestant and rationalistic sympathies. Next follow some quotations of the critical and liberal admissions of noted Modernists, in crude isolation from the context of the whole position. Then those Modernists are told that, though they are on the right track, they have not read history, or have read it to little purpose; that they cannot see the Papacy as it is seen by the clear impartial eye of a total outsider; that the Pope claims to be infallible and that it is idle to hope that he will ever accept and define the truth of Modernism. They will surely be excommunicated and the bark of Peter will pursue its even course towards the rocks as before. Let them give up their childish dreams, and courageously push on to the only possible conclusion, which the whole world discovered centuries ago. Then, with a pat on the head and a final benediction, they are good-naturedly dismissed.

Now this might be an excellent criticism of that Liberal Catholicism which is associated with the names of Lamennais, Lacordaire, Montalembert and, later, with that of Newman, and of those who followed his aims rather than his methods. But as a criticism of the former position of M. Loisy and of those who still adhere to it, it is entirely beside the mark. The former undoubtedly believed and hoped that the categories of existing Catholicism were elastic enough to accommodate themselves to the latest results of historical and critical research and to the requirements of modern life—ethical, economical and social. What they urged was, not a criticism, but an energetic development of those categories along the old lines without any change of direction. They did indeed entertain the hope (which no sane Modernist entertains for a moment) that some spiritual-minded Pope might one day, in spite of the bureaucracy that exploits his primacy as a political asset, approve and give force to their ideas. Any sort of revolution seemed to them incompatible with substantial continuity.

To the Modernist it does not seem so. Whether in the history of nations, or in the world of organic life, he recognises that such revolutions often belong to the normal course of development; that the larval life runs its course evenly, up to a certain point, only to prepare the way for a perfectly normal reconstitution. He is convinced that Catholic Christianity cannot live much longer on the old lines; that it has already reached a stone wall which it must surmount unless it be content to dwindle away as it is even now doing. The time has come, he thinks, for a criticism of categories—of the very ideas of religion, of revelation, of institutionalism, of sacramentalism, of theology, of authority, etc. He believes that the current expression of these ideas is only provisional, and is inadequate to their true values. He thinks that the Catholic Christian Idea contains, within itself, the power continually to revise its categories, and to shape its embodiment to its growth, and that such a transformation or revolution would be within the orderly process of its life—merely a step forward to a fuller and better self-consciousness from a confused and instinctive self-consciousness.

To suppose, then, that such Modernism is a movement away from the Church and is converging towards Liberal Protestantism is to betray a complete ignorance of its meaning—as complete as that of the Encyclical *Pascendi*. With all its accretions and perversions Catholicism is, for the

Modernist, the only authentic Christianity. Whatever Jesus was, He was in no sense a Liberal Protestant. All that makes Catholicism most repugnant to present modes of thought derives from Him. The difficulty is, not Catholicism, but Christ and Christianity. So far as other Christian bodies are true to Christ, they are faced by the same problems as are Modernists. If they escape them, it is because, in defiance of history, they have shaped Christ to their own image, and see in him no more than the Moslem sees in Mohammed.

The wisest men may be wrong, not only in detail, but in their whole scheme of things; yet they are not therefore fools. The Modernist's confidence in Christianity may be misplaced, but it cannot be despatched in a smart article or encyclical. We may be sure that religion, the deepest and most universal exigency of man's nature, will survive. We cannot be so sure that any particular expression of the religious idea will survive. Nay, we may be sure that all must perish, that none can ever be perpetual and universal save that which shall at last recognise and conform to the laws of the religious process, as they come to be established by reflection on wider experience. Should Christianity be unable, or unwilling, to conform to these laws, it must perish, like every other abortive attempt to discover an universal religion as catholic as science. Religion, however, will profit and learn by the failure. Fragments of the ruin will be built into some new construction raised on the old site—just as the ethics of Jesus have been built into the structure of Liberal Protestantism.

But the Modernist hopes for better things and thinks that he sees the principles of a true Catholicism in Christ and Christianity. Theoretically, it may be so. The difficulties, however, are mainly of the practical order, and men will differ in their estimate of their magnitude.

G. TYRRELL.

June 29, 1909.

PART I
CHRISTIANITY AND CATHOLICISM

CHRISTIANITY AT THE CROSS-ROADS

I

MODERNISM AND TRADITION

THE term "Modernism" is rapidly growing ambiguous. It was first applied, with hostile intent, to that group of Roman Catholics whose position was more or less travestied in the notorious Encyclical *Pascendi*. Next it was appropriated, rather reluctantly, by that same group, to stand, not for the travesty, but for the truth of their position. Then it was extended, quite legitimately, to like groups in the Church of England and other Churches, whose attitude towards tradition and modernity was analogous. In the ears of the public at large, which cares little about these controversies, it means what it sounds—modernity in religious thought; detachment from tradition; a new religion; a new theology; a new everything.

Of the avowed adherents or admirers of Modernism a large proportion understand it in this loose sense. They believe in modernity. Now a Modernist believes in modernity, but he also believes in tradition. If he criticises tradition, he also criticises modernity. In neither case is his faith blind. Of the two, his belief in tradition has a certain priority. It is his primary interest. A mere philosopher might be equally interested in showing that a properly criticised traditionalism is in harmony with a properly criticised modernity. But he could not therefore be called a Modernist. He might just as well be called an Antiquarian or Traditionalist. His interest is in the synthesis, but not in one more than in another of its terms. But, paradoxical though it sound, the dominant interest of the Modernist is in tradition. This paradox is due to the fact that Modernism has been christened by the ultra-Traditionalists, not by the ultra-Liberals. Newman was a reactionary for the Noetics, a progressive for the Ultramontanes. Of the two the Noetics were nearer the mark.

So, I would say, the attitude of the Modernist, however critical, is one of attachment to, not of detachment from, the Church's tradition. His attitude towards modernity, however open-minded and sincere, is one of detachment rather than attachment. So far as his affections are concerned he leans towards tradition; his concessions to modernity are reluctant.

I am dealing, then, with the Modernism of the Modernists, not with that of their adversaries on the right and left; nor with that of their undiscerning partisans and mistaken admirers. By a Modernist, I mean a churchman, of any sort, who believes in the possibility of a synthesis between the essential truth of his religion and the essential truth of modernity.

II

VARIOUS FORMS OF MODERNISM

THERE is obviously a practical and a speculative side to this problem, according as we consider the institutions or the teachings of the Churches on the one hand and those of the modern world on the other. Roughly speaking, it is a battle between Authority and Liberty; between Dogma and Science.

The practical problem is undoubtedly the more acute, complex and difficult. Under its pressure, both here and abroad, many have been led to abandon the Modernist hope and to turn away from the Churches to preach a new secular religion of life and progress to the alienated multitudes. They argue that, to be vital and effectual, a religion must express, while idealising, those moral and social aspirations of the people from which it originally sprang. All religions, they contend, originated in this way by the agency of priests or prophets, in whose minds moral and social ideals received a mystical interpretation and supernatural sanction, and became practically the law, the will of God. Even where a religion has been imposed from outside, by conquest or otherwise, it has taken root only so far as it could explain and sanction life as lived by the people in question, and thereby assist in the development of that life. Thus it was that Christianity obtained a footing, first among Jews, of whose life it was the product; then among Greeks, Romans and Barbarians, to whose life it was, in great measure, adaptable. They hold that, by a process of petrifaction and arrest, by the canonisation of the past, the ethical and social ideas of Christianity have ceased to be those of the new people, who have outgrown and departed from it; that the Churches and the Age differ even more profoundly and hopelessly in their conception and valuation of life than in their conception of truth; that a mental revolution were not nearly so impossible as a moral revolution. Believing that the Churches have thus lost all vital and vitalising power, all grip on the living and actual interests of the new world, all leverage for its movement, these thinkers would leave religion aside for the present, and preach all that is best, most ideal, most truly essential in the spirit of the age, trusting that, in course of time, its implicit religion will become explicit in obedience to man's imperious need of a religion.

To this highly philosophical scheme, I suppose,

a Modernist would reply that the disparity between the Christian conception of life and the modern conception, which has, after all, grown out of it, cannot be quite complete and absolute; that the new conception is by no means divine and needs criticism as much as the old; that the result of this double criticism would be to reveal a fundamental unity. He would allow the impotence of the Church, the irreceptivity of the age, but would ascribe them to accidental, not to essential, perversions.

But if it be hard to reconcile these opposites in thought, it is still harder to reconcile them in fact; and all that the Modernist has to urge against the more desperate and impatient solution is hope and patience. No two men will quite agree as to the precise moment when a case becomes desperate. It is a judgment that depends on differences of experience and temperament, and each must be left to the liberty of his opinion.

It is, however, with the doctrinal rather than with the practical Modernism that I propose to deal. Allowing that life and action, involving as they do a confused consciousness of the truths they imply, are more important than the analysis and statement of those truths in doctrinal form, yet a slow reaction of doctrine upon life and action cannot be denied. If the root affects the branches, powerfully and directly, the branches may affect the root, slowly and indirectly, but not less really. If our feelings govern our thoughts in a great measure, our thoughts, in a little measure, may gradually modify our feelings.

Moreover it is chiefly with Roman Catholic Modernism that I propose to deal, not merely because I know more about it, but because it is Modernism *par excellence*, the first to bear the name and pass it on to analogous movements.

In the Roman Church the problem attains its clearest statement, its greatest urgency. For, in the first place, her doctrinal positions, being far more numerous and daring than those of any other Church, offer a wider target to the shafts of criticism. Secondly, scholastic logic has bound these positions into a system so compact as to obliterate any distinction between fundamental and contingent elements. They all stand or fall together, for they are all attached to the one root of ecclesiastical inerrancy. Other systems, more loosely organised, could survive the amputation of this or that member; Rome would bleed to death if she sacrificed her little finger. Finally, this system, in its rigid unity, is tied fast, as none other, to certain fundamental presuppositions, which are assailed to-day by a philosophy based on the comparative study of religions, past and present.

Hence the opposition between old and new is more precise and acute in the Roman Church than in any other. There the question is put more clearly and exactly than elsewhere. But the answer must interest, and eventually decide, the fate of every other Church that shares any measure of the same dogmatic system and rests on the same ultimate presuppositions. If Rome dies, other churches may order their coffins.

Indeed, it is its preoccupation with these ultimate presuppositions that makes Modernism to be, in the words of Pius X, "the compendium of all heresies." Former heresies have questioned this or that dogma, this or that ecclesiastical institution. Modernism criticises the very idea of dogma, of ecclesiasticism, of revelation, of faith, of heresy, of theology, of sacramentalism.

Heretofore, as Mr. A. Leslie Lilley somewhere remarks, Christendom has been broken up by vertical sections. Now it is threatened with a horizontal cleavage, passing through all those sections impartially. There are not only Modernist Roman Catholics, but Modernist Anglicans and Nonconformists—nay, Modernist Jews and Mussulmans. Common to them all is the belief or hope that their respective Churches are not outworn, are not dead but sleeping; that the wine of Modernism is not so new as it seems, or else that the ecclesiastical bottles are not so old as they seem.

This criticism of religious categories and ultimate ideas has been slowly forced into existence by the detailed criticism of the results that have been deduced from those ideas. The need of reconciling these results with those of historical and scientific criticism has gradually driven apologists back to the very roots of religion, in their search for the exact point of divergence. Naturally, it is in the Church of Rome that the divergence has been most keenly felt and the search for its origin most eagerly prosecuted.

What is common to all Roman Catholic Modernists is the belief in a possible reconciliation of their Catholicism with the results of historical criticism. They differ widely as to what those results are, and as to the means of reconciliation. This reconciliation practically consists in a re-reading or reinterpretation of their Catholicism so as to find room in it for accepted facts; and also in an effort to control, and even resist, the destructive tendencies of criticism. Plainly this implies philosophising — a philosophy of Catholicism and a philosophy of criticism; and, as regards their philosophy, their reading of Catholicism, their reading of criticism, Modernists are of all possible varieties, shades and grades.

There are, as there always have been, men in the the Roman Church whose conflict with official orthodoxy springs, not from their historical, but from their philosophical convictions. One need only think of Pascal, Descartes, Malebranche, Lamennais, Gioberti in the past, as well as of Dom Romolo Murri, and of the Christian Democrats and Sillonists in the present, who are fighting for ethical, economical and political convictions, while repudiating all connection with theological Modernists and their historical problems. As the Church claims infallibility in morals as well as in faith, their orthodoxy is only partial at the best, and their conflict with her doctrinal authority is not less real because it concerns matters of conduct rather than matters of theology.

One must add to these another Category of Modernism, condemned by Pius X under the names of "Laicism" and "Presbyterianism," which consists in a protest against that progressive centralisation of the Roman Church, by which first the laity, then the priests, and finally the bishops, have been deprived of all active share in Church life and government; which demands constitutional guarantees for the liberty of the subject against the caprices of authority; and which is inspired by the idea of democracy as well as by a knowledge of the original constitution of the Church. This is the most widespread of all forms of Modernism, and is shared by thousands who would cordially anathematise Dom Romolo Murri as well as M. Loisy.

I must, however, confine my attention to theological Modernists and their historical problems.

Where there are so many shades and grades it will be well to take the problem in its most extreme and aggravated form. If a case can be made out for that form, the milder forms will be defensible *a fortiori*. If not, they may still be defensible on other grounds.

III

THE OLD ORTHODOXY

THE historical objections raised against official orthodoxy are drawn, first of all, from the study of the origin and development of ecclesiastical institutions and dogmas as excluding the traditional notion of immutability. Secondly, from the criticism of the Old and New Testaments—more especially of the Gospels, as conflicting with the Christological and various other affirmations of present orthodoxy. Thirdly, from the comparative study of religions as threatening the claim of Christianity to be the sole and absolute religion.

To estimate justly the measure of the difficulty we must be clear about the *terminus a quo* of Modernist criticism—about the claims of official orthodoxy. This is the more necessary as an illegitimate use of the category of development has been slowly introduced by way of a new patch to hide the rent in the old garment—and with the usual disastrous result. According to the orthodox theory, as defended by Bossuet, as assumed by the

Councils and the Fathers, the doctrines and essential institutions of the Catholic Church have been always and identically the same. The whole dogmatic, sacramental and hierarchic system, as it now stands, was delivered in detail by Christ to His Apostles and by them to their successors. He proclaimed, not the very words, but the very substance in all detail of the doctrines of Trent and the Vatican. He instituted the papacy, the episcopate, the seven sacraments. The Immaculate Conception of Mary was familiar, if not to the Patriarchs, as Pius X has taught us in one of his encyclicals, at least to the Apostles and the earliest Christians.

The Church is the infallible guardian of this system as delivered to her keeping by the Apostles —not to develop dialectically, but to preserve intact without addition or subtraction. "Keep the deposit," "keep the form of sound words"—that is her commission. It was an infallibility, not of new revelation or of further deduction and development, but of memory—of her collective memory. The Holy Ghost was to teach and bring to her remembrance all that Christ *had* said to her while on earth—nothing more. Hence in the early Church the appeal is always to the Past, not to the Future; the golden age of dogmatic truth lies behind, not before. Apostolicity, derivation from the Apostles through the Apostolic Sees, is the criterion of orthodoxy. It was not a question of what, logically, the Apostles *ought* to have held but did not hold; but of what they actually held. Novelty was the very definition of heresy. Deductions, which the Apostles had not imposed with the authority of revelation, could not be imposed merely on that of reason. Heresy was any departure from the actual and universal belief of the faithful. When such novelties arose and spread, bishops met in Council, not to debate an open theological question and impose their vote on the faithful, but to bear witness as to the actual faith of their flocks; not to decide what their flocks should believe for the future, but to declare what they did believe at present and had always believed; not to make the innovation heretical, but to declare that it was so already, as being a departure from the actual and morally universal belief of the faithful; not to define an open question, but to define that it never was open. They did not make the truth to be *de fide* but *de fide definita*—they defined that it was already *de fide*. In this view of unchanging tradition there was no real, but only a verbal, difference between the actual Christology of the Nicene and the ante-Nicene Church. The faithful may previously have said *homoiousios*, " of similar substance," but they meant *homousios*, "of identical substance"—all except a few heretical innovators. Against these the Council selected a term more accurately expressive of the universal and unbroken apostolic tradition. It did not make a new article of universal belief.

So too Pius IX did not decide the open question as to whether Mary's conception was or was not immaculate, as though it had not been always *de fide* and universally held. He only declared, against innovators, that the faithful with the exception of an insignificant minority had always, as well as everywhere, believed in the Immaculate Conception. If there were saints in this minority, such as Augustine, Bernard, Thomas Aquinas and Anselm, they were heretics in good faith, but none the less heretics, in opposition to the general belief of their contemporaries.

The Vincentian Canon sums up this view, in its criterion of faith, as that which is believed by everybody everywhere, and has always been so believed. Nor must we be misled by Vincent's apparent concession to development. For, in his physiology, the difference between the boy and the man is only that of implicit and explicit; not that of potential and actual. It is, like the evolution allowed at the Council of Florence, the difference between a cloak that is folded up and the same spread out. All that is revealed when it is spread out was there from the first, not potentially, but actually.[1]

Plainly this view of unchangeableness soon encountered difficulties, even in times to which the Past was sealed and its divergence from the Present almost wholly unsuspected. The way in which those difficulties were met supposes a conception of tradition wherein development could have no place. The only semblance under which later theologians have sought to shelter their theory of development is the distinction just mentioned between implicit and explicit belief; between the cloak folded and the cloak outspread. Because a deduced conclusion is "implied" in its premisses, no less than those premisses in the conclusion, later theologians have quietly interpreted *implicit*

[1] Driesch, in his *Gifford Lectures*, 1907 (p. 46), notes that, until the triumph of "epigenesis" in the eighteenth century, "evolution" meant in biology an actual, not merely a potential, pre-formation of the mature organism in its germ. Each part was there in microscopic proportions. But "true epigenesis in the descriptive sense of the term does exist. One thing is formed *after* the other; there is not a mere 'unfolding' of what exists already, though in a smaller form; there is no *evolutio* in the old meaning of the word." Under this confusion between evolution as an unfolding of actual packed-up parts, and evolution as epigenesis or growth of new parts contained virtually in a germ, recent theologians have claimed the authority of S. Vincent of Lerins and of the Council of Florence for an entirely new conception of doctrinal evolution, in flat contradiction to the ancient idea of doctrinal identity.

as meaning potential belief; whereas it had always stood for actual though not stated belief; for a belief too obvious to need statement; something taken for granted and never challenged.

If I say that I attended a friend's funeral it is not necessary to say that he is dead. That is stated implicitly. Yet it is not my potential, but my actual, belief; my actual belief in his death is implied in my actual belief in his burial. There are many more or less remote consequences of his death which I could, but do not, infer. These I believe potentially but not actually—i.e. I do *not* believe them. I may even deny them. *They* are implied, but *my belief in them* is not implied by my assertion of his death.

Against historical difficulties, drawn from the silence of earlier ages as to current beliefs, appeal was made, not to the potential, but to the actual, though implicit and unstated, beliefs of those ages. They were not mentioned because no one had challenged them; but had the man in the street been questioned he would have answered as the Church of to-day.

Another appeal, quite inconsistent with any theory of development, was to the *Disciplina Arcani* and to all that Christ taught the Apostles during those forty days after His resurrection. This was not written down, but was confided to the rulers of the Church to be dispensed according as exigencies might demand. All apparent additions to the Creed were, from the first, known explicitly to a favoured but undefined few, who transmitted them to the episcopate or to the Pope. How much more these know only the future can tell. This is hardly consistent with *quod ubique, quod ab omnibus*, though it saves the *quod semper*. As a weapon of apologetic it has been laid on the shelf and its place has been taken by development —a weapon which simply murders the system it would defend.

IV

THE NEW ORTHODOXY

THIS new weapon fitted well to hands that had been trained in the disputations and debates of the schools, where a man who held certain premisses might be forced, even against his will, to admit the conclusion that followed from them. He seemed to be thus convicted of holding what he did not hold or even denied—as though it had been buried and lost in his subconsciousness. At this rate earlier generations, who had admitted the premisses while denying the conclusions of later theologians, might be said to have admitted those conclusions by implication; and thus modern doctrines, in the face of such manifest and explicit denial in the past, might claim to have been held *semper, ubique, ab omnibus*. Thus S. Augustine, S. Anselm, S. Bernard, S. Thomas, while explicitly denying, implicitly believed the Immaculate Conception of Mary.

But it is one thing to say that the truth (or objective belief) was implied in their admissions; another to say that their belief in the truth was so implied. An implied potential belief is not the same as an implied actual belief. Under this ambiguity of the word "implicit" a new conception of tradition has been quietly substituted for the old. If a man is said to believe and admit, in spite of his explicit denial, all that is objectively implied by his data, then every avowed atheist is a theist, and every heretic orthodox. If S. Thomas was not a heretic for denying the Immaculate Conception, neither was Arius a heretic for denying the Godhead of Christ. It is irrelevant to say that the former dogma was not yet *de fide definita*, for it could not have been defined unless it had always been *de fide*, always accepted by the faithful at large. All we can say is that, in default of public definition, S. Thomas may not have known that he was an innovator and a heretic.

In this view, the whole character and meaning of an ecumenical council is changed. It becomes a theological debate. Bishops do not meet to bear witness to the constant and universal belief of their flocks, against some unheard-of innovation, and to prove it a heresy simply by showing it to be contrary to the actual universal faith. No; someone has started a new opinion which has gradually spread and divided the Church into two camps. So far it is an open question; the faithful are at perfect liberty to choose this side or that.

Those who choose the wrong side are not heretics, for there has been no definition. They are justified by their willingness to accept whatever a council may decide. In that willingness all orthodoxy is implied. In virtue of that willingness S. Bernard, while denying, really believed in the Immaculate Conception. When union and charity are threatened by the dispute, and the faithful are at their wits' end and do not know what to think, bishops meet for an ecumenical debate. They do not come to apply the criterion of universal and constant belief; for the opinion is new and the faithful are at sixes and sevens on the subject. They do not come to declare what is and always has been *de fide*, but to make something *de fide* for the future that was not so before and might be denied inculpably. They debate the question on its own merits and then impose their decision on the faithful as a law of belief, which is not new only because it lay potentially in the admissions of former generations, just as the first book of Euclid lies potentially in the axioms, postulates and definitions. It was always and universally believed by the faithful even when they denied it.

In the old view revelation was guarded by the infallible memory of the faithful collectively. To know what was of faith was not a question of speculation and argument, but of observation.

When communication was more difficult than now, it was possible to mistake local for universal beliefs. The point was decided by reference to the Apostolic Sees; especially to Rome, where Christians from all quarters came together; or else to a general council of bishops, who came to witness to the constant and universal belief of their several dioceses.

In the newer view revelation is guarded by the infallible understanding of the episcopate in ecumenical debate—infallible in deducing the logical consequences of the faith of past generations, and adding them to the ever-growing body of explicit and actual beliefs.

In the older view the body of actual beliefs was a constant quantity; in the newer it is susceptible of indefinite increase. It is frankly allowed to be far larger now than in the days of S. Bernard; far larger then than in the ante-Nicene Church. And yet it was always the same—not actually, but potentially, like the faith of an atheist who, from a potential, has become an actual believer. We are referred at every turn to acorns and oaks and grains of mustard-seed. The *Disciplina Arcani* is heard of no more.

As a means of explaining the ever-multiplying difficulties of history—its strange silences, its embarrassing affirmations—Development is a more elastic hypothesis than the *Disciplina Arcani*. We need not be astonished that earlier generations had not drawn out all the consequences of their admissions, or at times flatly denied those consequences; that they did not believe actually what they believed potentially. It was much harder to maintain that they were merely silent because the beliefs in question were too obvious to need mention; or because they were too sacred to be uttered publicly.

But this relief is purchased too dearly.

The fact that potential belief can consist with actual denial; that it levels all distinction between believers and unbelievers—since all are potentially believers—shows that it is not belief at all, any more than potential health is real health.

If this was what the Fathers and Councils meant by identity and immutability of doctrine, by *semper, ubique, ab omnibus*, why did they never recur to so obvious and easy an explanation, for surely the idea of dialectical development is as old as civilisation? It was not discovered by Darwin or Newman. No; the identity they taught was that of actual belief—of a constant body of doctrine from which nothing could be taken, to which nothing could be added; which was apostolic because it had been delivered whole and entire by the Apostles, not to the intellectual analysis, but to the unfailing memory or tradition of the whole Church. Their appeal was to the past, and not to the future, as the period of fullest enlightenment—an appeal inconceivable on the hypothesis of a development of Faith. All growth is from a formless germ to a plenitude of expansion; from the dimness of dawn to the light of perfect day. Its golden age is before it and not behind it; its criterion is its end, not its beginning. What would S. Paul, who lived in daily expectation of the Parousia, have thought had he been told that the light of Christian truth was but at its dawn; that he was living in the Church's darkest age; that even the nineteenth century would not see the sun at its height? What would the Christians of the first ages, with their faces towards the past, have thought had they been told that the fulness of revelation lay before and not behind?

This was too fundamental a point of tradition to be denied, and so we find the development theory clumsily tacked on to it. It is conceded that the Apostles knew fully and explicitly by revelation all that has been, or shall ever come to be, believed actually by the Church. But the sub-Apostolic age was not fit for this fulness of truth: only through long centuries could the Church be prepared to receive it. It was delivered to the sub-Apostolic age wrapped up in certain pregnant and central dogmas, whose potentiality has been unfolded by the divinely assisted dialectic of Christian thought. Thus dogmatic truth is slowly returning to that original fulness and explicitness which it possessed in the Apostolic mind. The process begins, as it ends, in a period of maximum illumination. From an initial maximum of evolution it passes immediately to a maximum of involution, and thence moves slowly and laboriously towards its original condition.

But if this fulness of Apostolic illumination was not communicable or communicated to the Church, how can we appeal to it? Of what use is it as a criterion if we are only to rediscover it at the end of time? The backward appeal can only be to the sub-Apostolic age—the age of maximum involution and darkness. And let us remember that the classical appeal was not merely to the Apostles, but to the earlier ages as nearer the plenitude of light, and therefore more enlightened.

Let us also remember that the Church claims to be the infallible guardian of that deposit of faith committed to her by the Apostles. Yet this hybrid theory of development implies that the casket of dogmatic jewels at once dropped from her weak and incompetent hands, and that she is infallible, not in keeping what she received, but in slowly recovering what she has lost.

But if such a theory of development is in flagrant contradiction with the patristic idea of doctrinal immutability, this patristic idea has long since crumbled to dust in the light of history. To find our present theological system in the first century is as hopeless as to find our present civilisation there. No one attempts it any longer. It was possible only for those early generations, whose divergences from the Apostolic age were comparatively slight, or for those later generations, from whom their palpable divergences from Apostolicity were hidden by their ignorance of the past. No Ultramontane pretends that the Immaculate Conception was actually and explicitly believed always and everywhere by everybody. They have transferred their cargo to the new vessel of development, whose unseaworthiness we have just noted.

Not that development can do more than postpone their shipwreck on the rocks of history. Even to show that the present doctrinal system was contained logically in the admissions of the first centuries means a torturing of texts and documents incompatible with any sort of historical sincerity. No historical probability, taken alone, is coercive, but the cumulus of probabilities is irresistible for all but the wilful sceptic; and under the weight of such a cumulus even the developmental view of doctrinal immutability falls to the ground.

V

NEWMAN'S THEORY OF DEVELOPMENT

THIS idea of dialectical development had long superseded the old apologetic of actual identity and unchangeableness when Newman appeared on the scene with the theory of doctrinal development associated with his name. The facts that it is thus associated with his name, and that it was vehemently opposed by the scholastic supporters of dialectical development, ought to be enough to prove that it is a radically different and irreconcilable system. That those who have condemned this system in the Encyclical *Pascendi* should try to show that Newman never held it, and that he was at one with scholastics in their purely dialectical idea of development, may be put down partly to tactics, and partly to ignorance and the tendency of the ill-read to read their own ideas into everything. The fact that Newman spoke of Christianity as the development of an "idea" easily misled those for whom "ideas" mean intellectual concepts, universals, definitions, from which a doctrinal system could be deduced syllogistically. Moreover his *Essay on the Development of Christian Doctrine* was undoubtedly written with one eye fixed on his scholastic critics, and with a view to dissemble the difference between their conception and his own as much as possible. His own conception, undistorted by any such synthetic effort, is to be found in his Oxford Lectures. It is one of biological, rather than of dialectical, development; organic, rather than architectural.

If a man is to be judged by what he is fundamentally, and in his dominant aims and sympathies, it is absurd to speak of Newman as a Modernist in any degree. It is equally absurd to speak of him as an Ultramontane; though it will be always possible for Ultramontanes to say that he was one until we have a sincere and integral publication of his correspondence. But if he was not an Ultramontane, it was because he was more, and not less, conservative than that *a priori* school which evolves history out of general ideas, and holds documents in abhorrence. The whole aim of his apologetic was the integrity of the Catholic tradition of the Roman Church; its preservation against the corrosive atmosphere of rationalism and liberalism. Yet the whole character and temper of his mind was adverse to the merely dialectical apologetic of scholastics and Ultramontanes, while his knowledge of early

Church history convinced him of the inadequacy of their attempt to reconcile primitive with present-day Catholic theology. He saw clearly that modern adversaries had to be met on their own grounds with their own weapons; that crossbows and bludgeons were helpless against long-range rifles.

What he did not see, perhaps, was the intimate connection between methods and their results; that the new could not defend the old, nor the old the new; that to give his adversaries the choice of weapons was to give them the victory. Here the instinct or intuition of the Roman Church, insisting on scholasticism as the only proper weapon of orthodox apologetic, is wiser. So far, and it is now very far, as the Roman system has been created by scholasticism, it can only be maintained and defended by scholasticism.

His Essay on Development is an *argumentum ad hominem*, addressed to the Tractarians. He uses his favourite method, derived from Butler: If you come so far, you must either come further or go back. If you are a Deist, you must become a Christian or a Rationalist; if you are a Christian, you must become a Catholic or a Deist. In short, if you are not a Roman Catholic, you must become a sceptic. So, too, if the Tractarians reject the later developments of Roman theology, why not also those of the Fathers and early Councils? If they can reconcile the latter with the Vincentian canon, why not also the former? In no case can the rigid and literal identity of the later and earlier theology with the *Depositum Fidei* be maintained. Development of some sort must be admitted. The original "deposit" must be conceived as in some sense a germ. To conceive it as a body of theological premisses, susceptible of indefinite dialectical development, would be obviously inconsistent with the appeal to the Apostolic age as the most spiritually enlightened. Theology and Revelation must be distinguished. The content of Revelation is not a statement, but an "idea" —embodied, perhaps, in certain statements and institutions, but not exhausted by them. This embodiment is susceptible of development; but the animating "idea" is the same under all the variety and progress of its manifestations and embodiments. There is a development of institutions and formulas but not of the revealed "idea," not of the Faith. Thus the advantage of later over earlier ages is merely secondary and protective—a compensation for their growing disadvantage. As time goes on the preservation of the original "idea" needs more complex defences against oblivion and distortion. As the initial force lessens, it needs to be husbanded more carefully.

In this notion of an "idea" as a spiritual force or impetus, not as an intellectual concept, Newman identifies himself with the modern, and separates himself from the scholastic, mind. It is the weapon that Modernists have taken from him and turned against much of that system in whose defence he had framed it. He himself must have owned that it was as far from the mind of the Fathers as from that of the scholastics; that when the Fathers spoke of the unbroken identity of the Faith, they were not thinking of an "idea" but of a dogmatic system, which neither had been nor could be developed —which had come down unchanged from the hands of the Apostles.

Dealing with Tractarians, he is more concerned about the "idea" of the Catholic Church than about that of Christianity. He assumes their identity as admitted by his opponents. He has merely to show that the "idea" of early and present-day Roman Catholicism is the same. He has to show that they are governed by the same ends, the same methods, the same temper —not always a very pleasant one—and therefore presumably embody the same idea of which even these unpleasantnesses are the characteristic, though morbid, manifestations.

As an *argumentum ad hominem* it is undoubtedly strong. But, for one whom it will drive forward, it will drive a hundred backward to reconsider the admissions that lead to such consequences. In virtue of his method Newman did as much for unbelief as for belief. Between himself and the sceptical issue stood the barrier of his own subjective and incommunicable religious experiences, and so his method carried him forwards and not backwards. Others may not share his religious experiences, or, if they do, may seek their explanation in psychology rather than in divinity; and for these his method is a two-edged sword.

VI

FIRST RESULTS OF NEW TESTAMENT CRITICISM

BUT the problem to which Modernists have to apply Newman's theory of Development is one which he saw only in vague outline, as a cloud on the distant horizon. He was contemporary with that application of historical criticism to Christian origins and to the New Testament which occupied so many German scholars in the nineteenth century. But Germany was further from Oxford in his day than at present, and he did not even read German. It was generally assumed, and comfortably believed, that this criticism, as the work of German rationalists and infidels, could offer no immediate danger to the belief of sensible people in this country; that the critics were all at sixes and sevens, so that any of their assertions could be met with counter-assertions from their own fraternity; that there was nothing but endless oscillation, no real progress, no established results; that at any rate the dispute was confined to the study and could never reach the street.

As a matter of fact it has reached the street and the railway bookstall, to a great extent here, to a far greater extent in Germany and elsewhere. Like every new subject of scientific inquiry, that of Christian origins gave rise at first to a whole chaos of conflicting opinions and hypotheses, but, as time went on, the number of issues was narrowed down steadily, and an amount of general agreement reached that seemed to justify the diffusion of such results in a popular form.

The problem of present-day Catholicism is, not to reconcile itself with that of the earlier centuries, to find in both a common "idea" of ecclesiasticism, but to find ecclesiasticism of any sort in Jesus Christ as He is given to us by historical criticism; to find in the earliest Catholicism a true development of the "idea" of Christ. So far as Newman's narrower problem is concerned his contentions have, in many ways, gained rather than lost at the hands of historical criticism. The antiquity of the leading features and principles of Catholicism has been pushed further and further back, till its beginnings are found in the New Testament itself. The hierarchy is felt in the Pastoral Epistles; sacramentalism in S. Paul; theology in the Johannine writings; ecclesiasticism in S. Matthew; the Petrine ascendency in S. Matthew and the Acts.

Taking their idea of Christianity from German Protestantism and Pietism, critics are not concerned to distinguish between the claims of Tractarianism and Roman Catholicism, or to defend the purity of the first six centuries against the impurity of the subsequent thirteen. They agree with Newman as to the continuity of "idea" governing the Catholic tradition from S. Paul to Pius X. I say "with Newman"—not with the scholastic or pre-scholastic view of continuity of the dogmatic and institutional system. Of these views their method is entirely destructive. It shows equally that there has been a continual process of growth, and that that growth has not been dialectical; but, like that of civilisation, unified by its end, its idea, its spirit. For them the problem is the transition from Christ to Catholicism. And here we have two schools— one affirming, the other denying, continuity of idea. The former is at once the older and the newer; and this for a reason that points to its permanence.

The Eschatological view, as it is called, was first formulated in a spirit hostile to Christianity, as known under the form of German Protestantism. The intention of this school was to represent Christ's central inspiration as an illusion, and Christianity as the outcome of a fanatical dream to show that what was of universal and permanent value in His ethical teaching was not, and did not claim to be, His own; that what was His own was not of permanent value since it was coloured through and through with His illusion as to the immediate end of this world and the coming of a new miraculous world, in which sin would be impossible and where ethics would have no scope. In a word, they wished to show that the German Protestant Christ never existed any more than the Roman Catholic Christ.

Against the haste and crudeness of this first formulation of the eschatological view, subsequent critics waged, for many years, a steady warfare in favour of what we may call the Liberal Protestant Christ. "Liberal," because the rejection of the miraculous and, to a very great extent, of the transcendent, *Jenseits*, was common to them with their opponents.

VII

THE CHRIST OF LIBERAL PROTESTANTISM

THE Jesus of the school of critics represented to-day by Harnack and Bousset, was a Divine Man because He was full of the Spirit of God; full of Righteousness. He came (it is assumed rather than proved) at a time when the Jews were full of apocalyptic expectations as to the coming of the Messiah, who was to avenge them of their enemies and establish a more or less miraculous and material Kingdom of God upon earth. He Himself seems to have shared this view in a spiritual form, translating it from material to ethical terms. As destined by a Divine vocation to inaugurate a reign of Righteousness, a Kingship of God over men's hearts and consciences, He felt Himself to be the true, because the spiritual, Messiah. With difficulty He trained a few of His followers to this conception of the Kingdom and the Christ. He went about doing good (even working cures which He supposed to be miraculous) and teaching goodness. The essence of His Gospel was the Fatherhood of God and the Brotherhood of man;

or else the two great Commandments of the law—the love of God and of one's neighbour; or else the Kingdom of God that is within us. True, these were platitudes of contemporary Jewish piety, and even of pagan philosophy. But Jesus drove them home to the heart by the force of personal example and greatness of character—above all, by dying for His friends and for these ethical principles. Of course He was, to some extent, of His time. He believed in miracles, in diabolic possession; above all, He believed in the immediate end of the world; and a great deal of His ethics, coloured by that belief, was the ethics of a crisis. But these were but accidents of His central idea and interest, in regard to which we may say He was essentially modern, so far as our rediscovery of the equation Religion = Righteousness is modern, not to say Western and Teutonic.

For this almost miraculous modernity the first century was not prepared. No sooner was the Light of the World kindled than it was put under a bushel. The Pearl of Great Price fell into the dustheap of Catholicism, not without the wise permission of Providence, desirous to preserve it till the day when Germany should rediscover it and separate it from its useful but deplorable accretions. Thus between Christ and early Catholicism there is not a bridge but a chasm.

Christianity did not cross the bridge; it fell into the chasm and remained there, stunned, for nineteen centuries. The explanation of this sudden fall—more sudden because they have pushed Catholicism back to the threshold of the Apostolic age—is the crux of Liberal Protestant critics. The only analogy I can think of is the sudden appearance of Irvingite Catholicism in the bosom of Presbyterianism.

The theory is curiously akin to that of the neo-Roman theologians. In both Revelation is suddenly eclipsed with the Apostolic age, to regain its primitive brilliance only after the lapse of centuries. Here it is the Immaculate Conception that is rediscovered; there it is the Fatherhood of God and the first principles of morality.

It was to the credit of their hearts, if to the prejudice of their scientific indifference, that these critics were more or less avowedly actuated by apologetic interests. They desired to strip Jesus of His medieval regalia, and to make Him acceptable to a generation that had lost faith in the miraculous and in any conception of another life that was not merely a complement, sanction and justification of this life. They wanted to bring Jesus into the nineteenth century as the Incarnation of its ideal of Divine Righteousness, i.e. of all the highest principles and aspirations that ensure the healthy progress of civilisation. They wanted to acquit Him of that exclusive and earth-scorning other-worldliness, which had led men to look on His religion as the foe of progress and energy, and which came from confusing the accidental form with the essential substance of His Gospel. With eyes thus preoccupied they could only find the German in the Jew; a moralist in a visionary; a professor in a prophet; the nineteenth century in the first; the natural in the supernatural. Christ was the ideal man; the Kingdom of Heaven, the ideal humanity. As the rationalistic presupposition had strained out, as spurious, the miraculous elements of the Gospel, so the moralistic presupposition strained out everything but modern morality. That alone was the substance, the essence, of Christianity—*das Wesen des Christentums*. If God remained, it was only the God of moralism and rationalism—the correlative of the Brotherhood of man; not the God of Moses, of Abraham, Isaac and Jacob; of David and the prophets.

Now it is clear that every scientific inquiry must be impelled by a motive and guided by a hypothesis. A method is in itself a dead tool without force or direction. Were truth not advantageous, the will could not seek it. The question is whether we are thinking of some particular, personal or party advantage or the advantage of human life as a whole; whether our desire is individual or universalistic in its interest—a desire of the separate or of the spiritual self. The weight of a given planet has no immediate bearing on practical politics, but only on the completeness of the human understanding, which is a co-factor of human life in general. Truth for truth's sake means truth for life's sake, it only excludes an eye to any less universal advantage. What we call "idle curiosity" is often a healthy instinct—a desire to integrate our general view of the world in which we have to live.

True, scientific inquiry cannot be coldly disinterested, but any other interest than the integration of knowledge distorts its vision. Here the Liberal Protestant critics failed no less than the positively anti-Christian critics. Their hypothesis was an article of faith, not an instrument of inquiry. If they have been beaten off the field we need not, perhaps, set it down to the severer detachment of their conquerors, but to the stricter application of that critical method which they invoked

It is by that method that Johannes Weiss and his followers have been forced back, very unwillingly in most cases, to the eschatological and apocalyptic interpretation of the Gospel. Very unwillingly, because it destroys the hope of smoothing away the friction between Christianity and the present age; because, in closing the chasm between the Gospel and early Catholicism, it makes the Christianity of Christ, in all essentials, as unacceptable as that of Catholicism.

Of this state of things Loisy was not slow to take advantage in *L'Évangile et l'Église*, directed against the Liberal Protestantism of Harnack's *Wesen des Christentums.* The Christ that Harnack sees, looking back through nineteen centuries of Catholic darkness, is only the reflection of a Liberal Protestant face, seen at the bottom of a deep well. Applying Newman's notion of development to a broader and deeper problem than Newman's, Loisy contends that the "idea" of Christ, in its substance and character, is identical with that of Catholic Christianity and opposed at nearly all points to that of Liberal Protestantism.

Rome (profoundly ignorant of the critical movement, its currents and tendencies) thought that even a victory over the Protestant might be purchased at too great a cost, and repudiated a notion of development different from that of her theological dialecticians, and disastrous to their idea of orthodoxy. Her hostility to the book and its author have created a general impression that it is a defence of Liberal Protestant against Roman Catholic positions, and that "Modernism" is simply a protestantising and rationalising movement. This confusion is widespread within and without the Roman Church, and many who account themselves Modernists are disciples of Harnack rather than of Loisy.

VIII

THE CHRIST OF ESCHATOLOGY

LET us consider for a moment the figure of the historical Jesus as it slowly emerges from the hands of criticism. We can only see it in dim outline, for it is incomplete in many a detail. But as it stands in the rough it is enough for our purpose. If the material is supplied by S. Mark, we cannot complete the image without assistance from S. Matthew and, to some extent, from the other evangelists.

There is no evidence to show that the Baptist and Jesus appeared at a time of high Messianic expectations and were, so to say, creations of their surroundings. Both seem to have been mystics and seers, the creators rather than the creatures of an epoch. Indeed, the whole attempt to write the Gospel story in the light of natural psychological laws, working in given social conditions, is doomed to failure. For the supernatural beliefs and intuitions of Jesus played the chief part in that story and interfered with the concatenation of natural causes. His Messianic consciousness was the main determinant of His action and utterance. Of that consciousness we do not know the source, presumably it was derived from some sort of vision or revelation. Inferences and inductions are not wont to be so tyrannically strong and irresistible. His Christhood was the secret, the mystery of His life. He revealed it reluctantly and cautiously to His disciples; He confessed it at His trial in order to induce His death; but otherwise and even from the Baptist He hid it away. Of anything like a development of His Christ-consciousness there is no evidence that will stand criticism. His eschatology was just that of the Jewish apocalyptics, with the difference that He Himself was destined to be the Son of Man. The Son of Man was a superhuman heavenly being, the ruler of a supernatural Kingdom of God, that was to descend upon earth and take the place of the present order of things. He was not the Messiah of the prophets, who was to secure the temporal supremacy of Israel on earth and reign on the throne of David. The decay of that prophetic hope had introduced the more radical apocalyptic hope. The Kingdom of God was not to be realised by any gradual development of the present order, but by an irruption of the supernatural order. While on earth Jesus was, in some sense, the Son of Man only by destiny. He had to wait for His glorification and manifestation. In what way He was to put on that higher nature is not clear. But the "possession" of human beings by superhuman beings, by the spirit of God or by evil spirits, was a familiar idea in those days. There is reason to think that He mingled certain elements of the prophetic Messianic expectation with the apocalyptic idea. His conception of the righteousness preparatory to entrance into the Kingdom was inward and spiritual, not legal and external. Probably He regarded Himself, in His earthly state, as the promised Son of David,[1] and the "suffering servant" who was to be glorified eventually as the Son of Man. Of the nearness of the final catastrophe He was convinced, His own advent into the world was guarantee for that. So far, and as far as He had already seen Satan falling from Heaven and the

---

[1] There is no reason to question His Davidic origin. The apologetic anxiety of Matthew and Luke, with their incompatible stories of His birth in Bethlehem, neither disproves the possibility that He was born there, nor that He was of Davidic stock. S. Matthew, as usual, is preoccupied about the fulfilment of a supposed prophecy as to the locality of His birth, not as to His descent. Had the claim (which was a very early one) to Davidic origin been mythical, it could easily have been refuted by reference to James and his other surviving kinsmen. When He asks how the Son of David can also be David's Lord, seated at God's right hand, He seems to hint at His own secret of the mysterious identification of the prophetic Son of David with the apocalyptic Son of Man—a veritable union of two natures in one personality.

demoniacs quailing before Him, He could speak of the Kingdom as already on earth—"even at the doors." It might burst forth in a year; it could not delay beyond a generation. His work on earth was to prepare and hasten the Kingdom —to close the last chapter of human history. He was here avowedly in the rôle of a prophet—the prophet from Nazareth; and being destined to shine forth as the Son of Man He was here incognito. He was here, not to preach His own glory—that, the Father would reveal in due time —but the coming of the Kingdom—His Father's business. From the days of the Baptist, and thenceforth, the Kingdom of Heaven was to be stormed and hurried on by prayer and repentance. Repent, He cried, for the Kingdom of Heaven is at hand. None but the righteous could enter in, or pass unconsumed through the fiery tribulations that were imminent—the wrath that was to come —or stand before the Son of Man in the approaching judgment.

Yet righteousness was not the substance of the Kingdom; eternal life was not the moral life. In the Kingdom men were to be as the angels of God; the moral struggle with all its conditions and occasions would be over, it would be rewarded by rest in glory, not by the glory of going on. Men would enter into the joy of their Lord, the

Son of Man—a superhuman, not a human, state. There is no hint in all this of a Kingdom of Christ, a reign of morality here upon earth to be brought about by the gradual spread of Christ's teaching and example. The parables of the mustard seed and the leaven, adduced in its favour, are irrelevant. They merely contrast the slightness of the cause with the greatness of the effect; man's natural efforts with God's supernatural response. Jesus did not come to reveal a new ethics of this life, but the speedy advent of a new world in which ethics would be superseded. Nor was His secret the fact that the expected temporal Messiah and Kingdom of Israel were parables of moral values. He thought of the Messiah and the Kingdom as did His contemporaries; neither as temporal, nor yet as moral, but as transcendental and supernatural. Men were to be transformed and glorified; heaven and earth were to be transfigured; the just were to eat the same spiritual meat and drink the same spiritual drink at the heavenly banquet with Abraham, Isaac and Jacob; there was to be no more death or sorrow or sin or temptation, for the former things were to pass away. The poor, the meek, the peacemakers, the merciful, the pure, the mourners, the hungerers after justice, the persecuted would be so no more; and their virtues would cease with their occasions.

The morality of Jesus was for this life, not for the next—the passing condition, not the abiding substance of blessedness. Nothing is original in the righteousness preached by Jesus. All is to be found in the prophets, psalmists and saints of the Jewish people, not to speak of the pagan moralists and saints. It represents but the highest dictates of man's purified heart and conscience. Much, however, is coloured by the immediate expectation of the end and is applicable only to such an emergency. In such a crisis it was not worth while to assert a thousand just claims that, in normal circumstances, could not be inculpably neglected. There was only time to seek the Kingdom of God in which all such losses would be made good.

Involved in the apocalyptic idea of the immediate advent of the Kingdom were three of its necessary preludes—the coming of Elias; the outpouring of the Spirit; the fiery tribulation through which the just were to pass to their glorification.

That the Baptist did not consider or announce himself as Elias is clear; not only from silence, but from his question to Jesus: "Art thou He that cometh?"—a term that referred to "that prophet" and not to the Son of Man, who was to appear in the clouds and was not expected first in human form. "Elias indeed cometh and shall restore all things"; here, as upon another occasion, Jesus reveals, in the form of a mystery or secret, that, in John the Baptist, Elias has already come—a secret connected with and dependent on that of His own Christhood. The Baptism of John was unto repentance and a new life. It was not a merely symbolic and ritual act, as we Modernists take for granted. The idea of sacraments or effectual symbols was as familiar to the Jewish as to the Hellenic mind of that day. It was dominant in the apocalyptic scheme, under the form of sealings and tokens. The Eucharist, as celebrated by Jesus, was not merely a figure but an effectual pledge of a participation in the Messianic banquet of the coming Kingdom. If Hellenic influences accentuated the sacramental idea later, it was none the less truly in the mind of Jesus. So too the Baptism of John was an effectual cause of the righteousness and repentance that entailed the subsequent baptism of the Holy Spirit, and the consequent transfiguration of the body in the Kingdom of God. The Christian Church carried on this baptism, with the difference that the Spirit, already poured out on earth, is at once given to the recipient of John's baptism.

The outpouring of the Holy Spirit, foretold by Joel as the immediate prelude of the Day of Judgment, had for its end the introduction of the new world and a transfigured humanity. Those who were "possessed" by God's Spirit were transformed essentially into Sons of God and new creatures; they were proved so by superhuman works, by dominion over devils and demoniacs, as much as by moral gifts and graces. Like those who were possessed, they spoke with strange tongues—the tongues of angels, not of devils. They were endowed with a preternatural wisdom that none could withstand and that no premeditation could assist: "For it is not ye that speak, but the Spirit of your Father that speaketh in you." It seems clear that Jesus considered Himself as "possessed" with the plenitude of this "Power from on high" from the moment of His baptism by John. For Him no intermediary stage of "repentance" was necessary. It was this Spirit that forthwith drove Him into a conflict with the Spirit of Evil in the desert. This was no mere moral parable, but a visionary experience; and visions in those days were not hallucinations but revelations of hidden realities. From this story we learn that Satan had usurped the dominion of the whole world, which was now to be wrested from him by a despoiler stronger than he. The fact that Jesus and His disciples cast out devils by the power of the Holy Ghost was a sign that the Kingdom of Heaven was at hand and the Kingdom of Satan overthrown.

It was probably not from the Heaven of the Blessed (where he is placed in the *Book of Job*) that Jesus saw Satan fall like lightning, but from the throne of the Prince of the Air, of the Ruler of the Darkness of this world, who boasted that he would set his throne above that of God. The whole battle was between the Kingdom of Satan and the Kingdom of God. The visible conflict in this world was, according to apocalyptic thought, the shadow or double of an angelic conflict between the hosts of Lucifer and Michael in the upper and spiritual world. After the final struggle and the overthrow of Satan, the just were to be gathered with the angels into the Kingdom of God, to which they were predestined from the foundation of the world; the unjust were to be gathered with the Devil into that everlasting fire and outer darkness to which they and the devils had been likewise predestined. Predestination is no innovation of the Pauline and Johannine writings, but belongs to the thought of Jesus.

The third prelude of the End was the last desperate and unparalleled struggle of Satan for the retention of his Kingdom; the uprising of all the powers of evil against Jesus and His saints; the great "peirasmos" or temptation; the "fiery tribulation"; the "wrath to come," through which the just were to pass and from which they were to pray to be delivered: "Bring us not into temptation, but deliver us from the Evil One"; "Pray that ye enter not into temptation." It behoved Him, it behoved all His saints, to suffer these things, and so to enter into their glory.

If the Lord's Prayer admits of a moral interpretation, its first sense is eschatological. It is the prayer of and for the Kingdom. "Thy Kingdom come" is its governing clause. "Thy will be done on earth as it is in heaven" has reference, not to the present, but to the new earth, where there will be no sin or possibility of sin, and where ethics will be superseded. Their daily bread is enough for those who, in view of the immediate end, have no reason to hoard for a distant future; whose first care is to seek the Kingdom, through repentance and forgiveness, and to persevere to the end through the coming temptation or trial.

When He sent forth His disciples it was in the belief (Matt. X., 23) that, before they had preached to all the cities of Israel and returned to Him, He would come in the clouds as the Son of Man. Whether He was to have passed to His glory through death and resurrection, or to have been caught up into the air and transfigured like Elias, is not clear. But S. Paul (1 Thess. IV., 13–17; 1 Cor. XV., 50–3) shows that the alternative was recognised in apocalytic thought. In His discourse He does not treat the disciples as missionary teachers, but as heralds of the End. He promises them the gift of the Spirit, which shall make them wiser than all their adversaries and triumphant over the power of the Devil. He foretells them that tribulations, temptations and persecutions will come, of which there was no indication in existing natural conditions, but which were entailed in His belief in the immediacy of the End, and, therefore, of its necessary preludes.

Except their dominion over the possessed, none of these predictions were fulfilled when the Apostles returned. For Jesus this was an indication that the Kingdom had to be stormed yet more violently. He would go forth and raise the Powers of Darkness against Himself and thus, by His own death, hasten the issue, and deliver from temptation those whose spirit was willing but whose flesh was weak. He would suffer in their place and give His life as a ransom for many. He would go up to Jerusalem and provoke the ministers of Evil to a final assault. Henceforth His life is a quest of that death which was to open the Kingdom of Heaven to all believers. Such a death would necessarily be the death of the cross, with all its concomitant ignominies. His predictions of it were founded on His resolve; that of His subsequent resurrection was founded on His Messianic self-consciousness. It behoved Him to suffer and so to enter into His glory. But His Christhood was still a secret, shared only by His disciples. It was to be revealed to the world only when He should have come in the clouds, vindicated by the Father, whose glory, and not His own, was the end of His earthly mission: "I have glorified Thee on the earth . . . and now glorify Thou Me, O Father."

It seems probable that the Apostles' vision of the Transfiguration preceded rather than followed the confession of Peter, and is alluded to in the words: "Flesh and blood hath not revealed it unto thee; but My Father." It was by no induction or inference that Peter had divined His Christhood; but by a supernatural vision. All that could be divined otherwise was that Jesus was a wonder-working prophet—possibly Elias; possibly, even, the promised Son of David. But these were human personalities; whereas the Son of Man was (in common acceptance) a heavenly and a supernatural being. His destined identification with that being was the secret of Jesus; a matter of revelation, not of inference. There is no convincing reason to question the authenticity of Matthew XVI., 17–19; since the word "Church" there may well stand, not for an ecclesiastical institution, but for the body of the elect or predestined which, in the Apocalypse of S. John, is compared to a building founded on the twelve Apostles; while the keys of the Kingdom, with their power of binding and loosing, are in character with the apocalyptic conception of the Apostles, as sharing the judicial function of the Son of Man at the last day, seated "upon twelve thrones judging the twelve tribes of Israel."

If Jesus plans the details of His triumphal entry into Jerusalem, in accordance with His Messianic secret, it is not as the Son of Man but, at most, as Elias, or as the Son of David, that He is greeted by the crowd.

In Jerusalem His work is one of provocation rather than of teaching. He openly assails the Pharisees and priests; He cleanses the Temple with an assumption of authority that is a challenge to theirs. The challenge is taken up and His death resolved upon. It was as the agents of the Powers of Darkness that the Jews crucified the Lord of Glory. It was Satan who put it into the heart of Judas to betray Him. All was predestined and predetermined. Most probably the subject of Judas's betrayal was the Messianic secret, which Jesus shared only with His Apostles—His claim to be the Son of Man, Who was to appear in the clouds. No two witnesses could be adduced against Jesus in support of such a pretension. One was not sufficient. Hence He is at last adjured and proclaims Himself to be the Son of Man. The very claim was blasphemy and merited death. As a prophet, or even as Elias, the crowd next day would have rescued Jesus; but when the priests went among them and revealed His secret they simply howled for the death of the blasphemer. So far as the Apostles entered into that secret, and were not shaken in their faith by the outcry of priests and people, they must have expected the resurrection and glorification of the Son of Man, which was part of the Messianic scheme. There is no reason to doubt that Jesus had predicted it to them or that they so understood His words: "I will not drink henceforth of this fruit of the vine until that day when I drink it new with you in my Father's Kingdom." There is no reason to doubt that they had visions of the risen Jesus.

Such then, roughly, is the figure of Jesus as it leaves the hands of a scientific criticism, unbiassed by the prepossessions of Liberal Protestantism. Of the Jesus Who came forward openly as the Messiah in a spiritual (i.e. a moral) sense, Who preached and exemplified the righteousness of the inward Kingdom of God, Who founded the Kingdom on earth in the form of a school of imitators and Who died solely as a martyr of morality, there is not left a single shred. He did not oppose a moral to a worldly interpretation of the Kingdom. He took the current interpretation as He found it, which was not worldly but other-worldly—spiritual, in the sense of metaphysical and transcendent, not in the immanental moral sense.

I am not in a position to criticise and judge between these two readings of the Gospel. But if the value of a hypothesis is to be rated by the number of phenomena that it unifies and puts in their place, it does not seem to me that there is much choice left, or that the prolonged battle of Liberal Protestantism against the eschatological interpretation has done more than establish the superiority of the latter. There is, of course, a residue of difficulties, but they are few and small compared with those of the other hypothesis. Moreover, they are easily accounted for by the same tendency on the part of the redactors of the synoptics that gave birth to the ethico-spiritual Gospel of S. John. As the Kingdom tarried, it became more necessary to dwell upon the preparatory righteousness than on the Kingdom itself; to consider the expectant Church on earth as a Kingdom of Righteousness. It is, on the other hand, impossible to understand the introduction of the apocalyptical conception if such a Kingdom of Righteousness on earth had been the central interest of Christ's mission. Moreover, as a fact, this inward righteousness, which, though not original, was systematised by Jesus and enforced by the whole impetus of His inspiration, is the only sensible result of the Gospel. It has leavened and transformed humanity, slowly perhaps and partially, yet far more rapidly and fully than it could have done had it not been associated with a great religion. It is not then wonderful that, even in the Churches, while the once central interest of the coming judgment has dropped into the background, if not altogether into oblivion, the incidental moralism of the Gospel should stand out as its principal value, and the central apocalypticism be overlooked as a troublesome accident. And this tendency, in an age that repudiates the miraculous and distrusts the transcendent, can only be accentuated by those whose aim is to secure the sanction of Christianity for the best ideals of the time; to alleviate the friction between religion and reason as much as possible; to transform what was at most an ethical religion into a religious ethic.

IX

THE CHRIST OF CATHOLICISM

WE must now try to get hold of the "idea" embodied in the apocalypticism of the Gospel and compare it with that embodied in Catholic Christianity, to see whether they are merely different embodiments of the same, and whether the latter can be considered as a development of the former.

Plainly we must distinguish between the substance or content and the form or expression of an "idea." As we use the word here an "idea" is a concrete end, whose realisation is the term of a process of action and endeavour. It is akin to that Augustinian *notio* (or *ratio*) *seminalis*, with which every living germ seems to be animated, and which works itself out to full expression through a process of growth and development. It does not change in itself, but is the cause of change in its embodiment. Transferred from the realm of organic life to that of human activity, an "idea" is still a good or end to be realised and brought to perfect expression. But it is rather a volition than a concept. Every volition, however blind and instinctive, is directed by the idea of an end to be reached. That idea is implied in the volition, but it is not necessarily given to the clear consciousness of the person who wills. Animals obey instincts without any knowledge of the ends with which they are pregnant. The meaning of many of man's spiritual and rational instincts is revealed to him only gradually, as he follows them step by step. In most cases their full meaning will never be clear to him. Thus civilisation, education, society, liberty, justice, are spiritual instincts with man. He does not start with a clear conception of what he wants; but his conceptions grow clearer, more explicit, more complex, more organised, as he moves along. In the embodiment or expression of the idea we must, then, include its intellectual expression or form.

Thus man's religious idea is first felt as a vague need of adjusting his action to that whole, of which all but a little part is hidden from him; of coming to terms with an invisible and mysterious world. This "idea" is the soul of the lowest and of the highest forms of religion. But the conception of the invisible world and its denizens, of its relation to man and the visible order, of the conduct by which the adjustment is to be effected, belongs to the embodiment or expression of the idea. It is determined by the idea and its environment—the intellectual, moral and social conditions of man. Its only criterion and corrective is the idea itself, which is no practical corrective since man only apprehends it in the very form that needs correction. His measure is at fault and cannot be tested by itself. But the idea, like Nature, eventually heals itself and asserts itself triumphantly over all obstacles. Thus, too, men long for liberty, but their very conception of liberty sends them on the wrong track till, coming up against a blind wall, they are forced back to the point whence they went astray. Hence we may not press the analogy between organic development and that of an idea so closely as to imply that the whole series of its embodiments is predetermined, like the stages of an organic process, of which each is required by or requires the next. Nor even where we do get an unbroken series of ever fuller expressions of the same idea does this exclude the possibility or actuality of other quite different series. Thus the idea of liberty, in different times and places, has been productive of various processes of self-embodiment, with nothing in common but their many-sided and inexhaustible idea. The same is true of man's religious need and of the religious idea, which branches out in a thousand directions, in search of an essentially unattainable completeness of expression.

By the "idea" of Jesus I mean, then, the religious idea in a certain stage of development, along a particular line. I ask myself: Is Catholic Christianity on the same line, or, as Liberal Protestants suppose, on an entirely different line? Is it the outgrowth of the same branch, or did it fork off in the first century? Is it simply a Hellenic process, violently grafted into the Liberal Protestantism of Jesus—the latter being interrupted at that point until the graft was broken off by criticism?

Now so far as we find an actual identity of form and category we are plainly justified in supposing the same idea to be at work on the same line. No doubt the expression or form is more ample and complex in Catholicism than in the Gospel, but its main and central features are the same.

Transcendentalism, or other-worldliness, belongs to the idea of religion as such, but in varying degrees. The whole tendency of Liberal Protestantism is to minimise the transcendence by establishing a sort of identity of form between this life and the other. So far as man's life is moral, it is an eternal life. The moral life has mystical and transcendental roots. It postulates a spiritual principle and end in Nature which we may call God. Heaven and the Kingdom of Heaven are in our midst; they are the spiritual or moral side of life.

Without this concession to transcendentalism, Liberal Protestantism would not be a religion at all. As it is, it is rather a system of religious ethics than a religion. It merely insists that morality is religion and adjusts our life and action to that spiritual and invisible side of the world which is an object of faith, a necessary postulate of morality. No doubt this is a truth of Christianity; but not its whole truth. Emphasis is laid on it in the Fourth Gospel; in the synoptics it is implicit rather than emphatic. Christ had not come to emphasise the religion and the revelation implied in righteousness that were within the reach of man's reason. His emphasis was on the other-worldly, supermoral life of the coming Kingdom. How could it be otherwise on the very brink of the destruction of the present order? What need of a new ethics for expiring humanity? His whole emphasis, therefore, was on the other world, and on the conditions by which men might attain it and flee from the wrath to come. Of these, repentance and true inward righteousness were the chief. But men did not so much need to be told what righteousness was, as to be called back to it or converted to it. And this Jesus did by giving the will a motive: "Repent ye, *for* the Kingdom of Heaven is at hand."

If, then, the religion of Jesus was not exclusively

transcendental, its emphasis was almost entirely on the other world—the world that is least present to man's mind and most easily forgotten. And this excessive transcendentalism is the great reproach made against Catholicism by the Liberal Protestant, as well as by the Positivist. It is true that the *immediacy* of the End very soon dropped out of Catholic consciousness, and so restored the depressed value and importance of the present life. But the belief in the End; in the eventual appearance of the Son of Man in the clouds; in the general Judgment and its preceding tribulations; in the destruction of the present order; in a transcendental and eternal Heaven and Hell, figures as the final and, in a sense, dominant article of her creed.

In her Advent liturgy one finds even the note of immediacy; though naturally it evokes no response in her consciousness. The contention that this immediacy was not essential to the idea of Jesus is not without plausibility. The words "Of that day or that hour knoweth no one, not even the Son," although consistent with a certainty that the End would be very soon, and within a generation, at least disclaim any sort of revelation on the point, and imply that any prediction can be no more than a private conjecture. The foreshortening of time in the prophet's mind does not affect the substance of the situation. The supposed near approach of death will often make a man reorder his life, as he ought to have reordered it in any case, in view of the certainty of eventual death. The scare has not given him a new reason but a new stimulus. It has made him attend to what he should have always seen. The public scare at the thought of the immediacy of the Kingdom, that all expected eventually, acted similarly. The Kingdom, not the immediacy of the Kingdom, was the reason for repentance, detachment and righteousness; the immediacy was but a stimulus to rouse the sluggish imagination—to change a "notional" into a "real" assent. Hence it may be said that the conception of immediacy was no part of the idea of Jesus; it was a supposed circumstance of the situation in which that idea was applied.

If Jesus Himself, as seems likely, experienced one or more disappointments in the matter, we cannot say that the further disappointments of His Church were for Him outside the range of possibility. Still those who now expect the End at all no longer expect it immediately, and have given up speaking of "those last days." Only now and then is there a recrudescence of apocalyptic panic in times of earthquakes, comets, wars and pestilences.

Christianity is, perhaps, the better and not the worse for the loss of this stimulus, to which it owes its birth. For the violent detachment, justified by such an expectancy, is hurtful to the duties and lawful interests of social life. No man who believes he has but a day to live will make proper provision for his future years. The scare may be useful to make him amend his ways. But a sustained scare would paralyse his energies. This evil was soon felt by the early Church in a certain anarchy and neglect of plain social duties. It was not worth while to assert the claims of justice, to establish and provide for a family. Men pooled their wealth and lived in the clouds and in idleness. "If any will not work neither let him eat" was a rebuke levelled against this state of things.

Yet this contempt of the world preached by Jesus was not Buddhistic in its motive. It was a contempt of a lower and transitory form of existence in favour of a higher — a proximate pessimism but an ultimate optimism. That the world was thought to be in its death-agony made it doubly contemptible. But when this thought was dropped by the Church, the world still remained contemptible. It was but a preparation and purgatory; the ante-chamber of Heaven; the theatre of the great conflict between the forces of good and evil—a conflict that could be decided in favour of Good only by the Coming of the Son of Man. It was a world in which the Christian was but a stranger and a pilgrim, looking for a City whose builder is God. The notion that Good was to triumph by an immanent process of evolution never entered into the "idea" of Jesus or of the Church.

But the impression of the first days remained with the Church long after the immediate expectation of the End had ceased: what Christ had said, what the early Christians had done in view of that immediacy, has lingered on as a rule of life, in diminishing measure, even to the present day. It was this excessive otherworldliness, which enters largely into the monastic and ascetic idea of Catholicism, that provoked that revulsion, which began with Luther and ended with the purely ethical Christianity of the Liberal Protestant, for whom the Kingdom of Heaven is but the ideal term of the moral evolution of man on earth.

To this ethical idea of the Kingdom some colour is given by the early tendency to view the Church as the Kingdom of God upon earth in a certain anticipatory sense—a tendency that appeared when men had ceased to look on the Heavenly Kingdom as imminent. Nor was it without warrant from Christ, who considered that, in Himself and in the Baptist, and in the victory of God's Spirit over the Devil, the Kingdom had already begun to touch earth. This conception of the Church, as the Kingdom *in fieri*, prepared the way for that of a moral humanity as the Kingdom. But the conceptions are radically distinct. Here a natural evolution is to complete the work; there, a supernatural cataclysm.

Again, the emphatic Persian dualism of Good and Evil, of the Kingdom of God and of that of Satan, is common to the idea of Jesus and the idea of Catholicism. The Devil is essential to the Catholic scheme. Renunciation of the Devil and his retinue (*pompa*) is the preliminary of that Baptism which enlists a man in the service of the Kingdom. Till then he is possessed by Satan, in virtue of his natural birth. This is the teaching of Jesus no less than of S. Paul or S. Augustine. Satan is exorcised to make room for the Holy Spirit. Every priest is an ordained exorcist, and exorcism has its prescribed ritual. A host of mental, moral and physical evils, which science now deals with, not to speak of storms, plagues and other destructive phenomena of nature, have, till quite recent times, been ascribed to the Devil by the Church, and treated by prayer and exorcism. Even so modern a

Pope as Leo XIII accepted the fables of Leo Taxil and his mythical Diana Vaughan, and exorcised Rome daily; and the prevailing mind of uncritical Catholics is still quick to explain all the evils of the time by the Devil and his human agents—Jews, Freemasons, Protestants and Modernists. The Devil introduced sin and mortality, with all their attendant evils, into the world.

On the other hand, with Christ came the fulness of the Holy Ghost poured out on all the baptised. Possessed by this Divine Spirit, the baptised becomes " a new creature " by an inward transformation of his nature. Ethical perfection is the congruous fruit but not the substance of that change. He is not divine because he is moral, but moral because he has become divine. So, too, the main fruit of all the sacraments of Catholicism is not the moral life of the present, but the supermoral life of the future. They, as it were, store up potential glory in the soul, which shall be liberated by death. Hence the contention that a life of very average morality, with frequent sacraments, is more pleasing to God than a life of heroic morality, without sacraments. It is only the sacraments that make us sons of God. Morality can never do so. It is but the congruous natural condition of grace, and gets all its lustre and merit from grace. Thus the baptised infant, incapable as yet of moral life, is made a divine creature by the expulsion of the Devil and the introduction of the Holy Ghost. In virtue of this new nature man is made immortal by a quasi-natural necessity. If he dies before the End he will rise in a spiritualised body; if he lives to the End he will be transformed and caught up in the clouds. As the Fourth Gospel says, he *has* eternal life in him already. Like Christ on earth he is only waiting for the eventual manifestation of the glory that is in him. Grace is the germ of glory. As little as the natural world could grow into the transcendental Kingdom of God, so little could the natural man, by a process of moral development, grow into a son of God, a spiritual immortal being. In both cases the change—a veritable transubstantiation—is effected by an irruption of the transcendental into the natural order; by a triumph of the Spirit of God over Satan. It is not a work of nature, but of unmerited grace.

Uncongenial as this dualism is to our modern minds, is it possible to deny that it is common to Jesus and Catholicism? It is not between Jesus and Catholicism, but between Jesus and Liberal Protestantism that no bridge, but only a great gulf, is fixed.

It is, however, a dualism between spirit and

spirit rather than between matter and spirit. This latter dualism came from the further East, and, through Hellenic philosophy, has left its traces in the Paulo-Johannine writings. But it was no part of the Jewish and synoptic tradition. Here, too, the Church has been faithful to the idea of Jesus in opposition to Gnostic and Docetan tendencies. For her, as for Him, the body is, by nature and by original destiny, the servant and not the foe of the spirit. Both were to be glorified. The new body and new world were to be made out of the old by a process of miraculous transfiguration. The mortality of the Son of David was to put on the immortality of the Son of Man. And so, throughout, the material was to be made the instrument, the sacrament or effectual symbol of the spiritual and transcendent.

For Catholicism as for Jesus baptism is no idle symbol, but an effectual cause of the new life of the spirit, and of that Divine Sonship which gives right of entrance into the transcendent world. As for the Church, so also for Jesus, the bread of blessing is the bread of eternal life, the antidote of death, the food of the angelic nature. Sacramentalism was a principle of Jewish as of all ancient religions, to which the miraculous was no scandal, since they knew nothing of a mechanically determined nature. In the absence of all proof of sacramentalism in the thought of Jesus, we should need positive and convincing proof that He did not share that idea with His religious surroundings.

And so as to externality and ritual in worship. Liberal Protestants are satisfied that He swept it away for a "worship in spirit and in truth"—as though there were an incompatibility between the two. They assure us that, were Jesus to come on earth, He would be quite at home at a prayer meeting, and quite at sea at a high mass. This is profoundly uncritical and unhistorical. He might say, perhaps, "This is your synagogue; now show me your temple"; or, "This is your temple; have you no synagogues?" From first to last Jesus revered and practised the religion of His fathers. As to the Divine authority of its moral and ceremonial law, even to the last jot and tittle He is at one with the Pharisees. He differed from them in emphasis; in the stress laid on the spirit as opposed to the letter, on the end as controlling the means. In this He had no consciousness of attacking but of defending the true tradition. He never hints at the idea that His followers are destined to break away from Israel: nor did they ever do so by any definite act of separation. During His life they were in the Jewish Church as the Wesleyans were once in the Church of England—a school of pietists, whose aim was to purify, not to abandon, their Church. Naturally we do not hear much in the synoptics of what is taken for granted—of His scrupulous observance of the Jewish religion; but only of the new piety and its practices. But it is preposterous to suppose that His insistence on inwardness meant a repudiation of outwardness, or a puritanical sense of opposition between them. By nature and by original destiny the bodily was for the service of the spiritual, however easily sin and Satan might pervert it from its end. Even the transcendent world of the Kingdom was not purely spiritual in the Hellenic sense. It was embodied, as glorified humanity was embodied. However refined and etherealised, it was sensible and phenomenal; nor was the Messianic banquet a mere parable of moral values. He did not say that He would destroy the Temple, but that, were it destroyed, He would raise it up again. When He purged it, He did not rend the veil or throw down the altar and its ornaments, saying: "Take these things hence." He drove forth those whose traffic dishonoured the sanctity of what He recognised as a house of prayer for all nations.

When, by the course of events, His followers were driven forth from the Jewish Church, it is not to be supposed that they ceased to recognise the need of a Church and of public worship, or were content with informal piety. If the Temple-worship entered into the religion of Jesus, a similar idea of worship belonged to the early Church, and was gradually realised by borrowings from Jewish and Hellenic sources. While the End was still felt to be imminent this externalism was but rudimentary and incoherent; later it became what it remains to this day. Naturally the worship at S. Peter's is not the worship of the Temple; but it is of the same type and belongs to the same idea, which was that of Jesus and His Apostles. In this respect, too, the Catholic Church is identical and continuous with the Apostolic band that Jesus gathered round Him. Its later independent organisation and externalism were contained in the idea of Jesus. There is no chasm; no need for a bridge. The temporary disorganisation of Apostolic Christianity, consequent on its separation from Judaism, was an abnormal state of affairs. The "idea" was bound to reassert itself as it did. Of that reassertion Liberal Protestants speak as of a deplorable relapse into the legalism from which Christ had made us free. What Christ freed us from was not externalism, but its abuse; not the letter, but its oppression of the spirit; not the priesthood, but sacerdotalism; not ritual, but ritualism; not the Altar, but the exploitation of the Altar. Here there has indeed been a relapse, but not more scandalous than the general relapse from righteousness and inward spirituality, due to the loss of belief in the immediacy of the End. When the Lord delays His coming His servants wax wanton or slumber.

Again, in the conception of Eternal Life as a supermoral life, as a state of rest after labour, of ecstatic contemplation of the face of God, Catholicism is true to the idea of Jesus and of the Apocalypse, as already stated. Liberal Protestantism is more anthropomorphic. So far as it admits another life at all, it is the strenuous life of the moral hero continued to all eternity—although in conditions that rob every known human virtue of its occasion and subject-matter. It seeks only "the glory of going on and still to be." For Jesus the moral is not the highest life but its condition. Eternal life is, undoubtedly, the reward or wages of righteousness, as Hell and Death are the wages of sin. This too has always been the Catholic idea; though the reward is only for those who are truly righteous, i.e. who love righteousness for itself and independently of the reward. In a word, it must be an inward righteousness of the heart, not only an outward righteousness of the hand. Neither the fasting nor the almsgiving of the Pharisees were condemned, but their self-complacency and consciousness of merited reward.

To regard the Communion of Saints as an exclusively pagan importation is again gratuitous. For Jesus, Abraham, Isaac and Jacob, Moses, Elias and David, were not of the dead past but of the living present. The blood of all the just, from Abel onward, who had been martyred by Satan's emissaries in the cause of God, was ever crying aloud for that vindication which was to be effected at the coming of the Son of Man. The tribulations of the Saints were to hasten that day and take the Kingdom of Heaven by storm, and this in union with and through the merits of His own blood. And in the Kingdom it was with Abraham, Isaac and Jacob that the redeemed were to sit at meat. Whatever the extension, ramification and superstition of Catholic saint-worship, it is idle to deny that it pertains to the "idea" of Jesus.

Nor can it be contended that, whatever explicitness it may owe to S. Paul, the sacrificial aspect of the Eucharist is alien to the thought of Jesus. If it be true that it was with the purpose of hastening the coming of the Kingdom that Jesus, after the return of the Apostles, went forth to provoke His death at Jerusalem, that death was in His mind a sacrifice for the benefit of the elect, and a ransoming of many from the thraldom of Satan. Even if the words: "This is My Body; this is My blood" were but a Pauline amplification of His thought, suggesting a parallelism with the pagan sacrifices, they were a justified amplification. If the bread and wine were truly sacramental tokens or sealings, effectual symbols and pledges of a participation in the future banquet of the Kingdom, every repetition of the rite must have been a commemoration and pleading of that death, which was to hasten the Kingdom with all its attendant benefits for the redeemed. It must have been viewed as a hastening of the day when they were to celebrate it with Jesus in the Kingdom of God; as a showing or pleading of His death till He should come. If this be so, then the centrality of the Eucharist in Catholic worship is true to the "idea" of Jesus. It is something far more than a mere reminder to the communicants of their Teacher martyred in the past, or a pure symbol of moral fellowship with Him and His true disciples. What the Liberal Protestant calls the "magical" conception of that sacrament belongs to the "idea" of Jesus.

Finally, when we turn to the personality and nature of Jesus Himself, we find that His own idea and the Catholic idea are at least closely akin, while that of Liberal Protestantism is another idea altogether. We find two natures—that of the earthly Son of David and that of the Heavenly Son of Man—mysteriously united in one personality. We find an earthly period, in which only one nature is manifest, opposed to a period of glory in which both are to be manifest. It would be at least hard to show that, whatever Catholic theology may mean by the doctrine of a hypostatic union from the very first of these two natures, that doctrine is excluded by the notion that Jesus was *made* the Christ only by His glorification after death. For Christhood may have meant the state of manifestation; and in this sense Jesus may have considered Himself as but destined to be "made" or declared the Son of Man through death. For Jewish thought the union would be conceived as a sort of "possession" of the lower by the higher nature. The distinction of *ousia* and *hypostasis* would have had no meaning.

As the just already possessed eternal life virtually at their baptism, so Jesus may well have considered Himself in a like virtual possession of His Christhood before it was actually made manifest — to have been thus virtually the Son of Man from the very first. This the more, as predestination was no mere purpose in the Divine mind, but something stamped in the very nature of the predestined. It was a seal, a token, imprinted on the soul.

It was certainly not in a moral and adoptive sense, but in a natural and metaphysical sense that Jesus claimed to be the Son of God by the fact that He claimed to be the Heavenly Son of Man. He was conscious of differing, not only in degree but in kind, from even the greatest of prophets. If the redeemed were His brethren, it was in virtue, not of their moral, but of their supernatural life, which they derived from and through Him, who had given them power to be made the sons of God. This power was the spirit—the seed of eternal life sown in baptism and blossoming in the Kingdom. Righteousness was the condition of its reception and retention, but was not the substance of Divine Sonship.

The position of Jesus in humanity is unique in kind. Not only is He the giver of participated sonship to others. He has come as God's plenipotentiary and vicegerent, at the end of time, to bring the world to an end, to judge the living and the dead, to separate light from darkness, tares from wheat, and gather the fruits of time into the garner of eternity. In virtue of His double nature He stands mediatorial between God and man. He is the Gate, the Way, the Truth, the Life, through which alone men can have access to the Father.

If, in her endeavour to fix the relation of Christ's heavenly nature to that of the Eternal Father, the Church may seem to have exaggerated the known claims of Jesus, this cannot be said of the Johannine and Pauline Christology, in which those claims are rather amplified than heightened.

Altogether it must be owned that, between Christ's idea of Himself and the Catholic idea of Him, there is no practical or substantial difference.

On the other hand, to maintain that it was only as a righteous man that He claimed to be the Son of God in a pre-eminent degree; that the Hellenic mind misunderstood this Hebraism and leaped at a bound to a belief in His Godhead, is almost grotesquely uncritical. Such convulsions of thought do not take place in silence or in one night. If the claim of even the best of men to be of a heavenly nature was blasphemy in the ears of the High Priest, and of the crowd that turned against Jesus when they heard of it, it would have been blasphemy in the ears of the early Church had it been an innovation. The supposition of such a chasm between the Paulo-Johannine Christology and that of the Synoptics is not credible.

Closely connected with the mediatorial nature and function of the earthly heavenly Jesus, Son of David and Son of God, is the doctrine of the Atonement wrought by His death—a doctrine which Liberal Protestantism attributes to S. Paul. Yet it is really inseparable from the apocalyptic idea of the Kingdom of God. The long battle between Satan and Heaven for the possession of the world and man was to culminate in a final and unparalleled outburst of the Powers of Evil and Death against the saints of God, through whose sufferings and perseverance God would be provoked to arise and scatter His enemies and establish His Kingdom. Jesus speaks of the blood of the just, from Abel onwards, pleading for vindication. In the Apocalypse of S. John the martyrs cry: "How long, O Master, the holy and true, dost Thou not judge and avenge our blood?" But the culminating crime of Satan, the crowning merit of suffering Righteousness, was the death of the destined Son of Man. This filled up the measure of Satan's iniquity and paid the full price of God's grace and mercy. Through the blood and suffering of Jesus the blood and suffering of the just became effectual to make atonement. Satan was bought out, his rights over the world forfeited, his slaves set free. So great was the crime, so great the merit of the death of Christ, that this alone would have sufficed to bring the Kingdom of God from Heaven to earth. The sufferings of the saints became, in a way, supererogatory. The great persecution could be shortened and mitigated for the sake of the elect. Hence, in every sense, His death was an atonement, a ransom for many; His blood was shed for many for the remission of sins. Thus we find a substantial agreement between the apocalyptic doctrine of Jesus and the theological doctrine of Catholicism. When we remember that Purgatory is only a displacement of the fiery trial that was to purify the saints, the shortening of Purgatory, through the supererogatory sufferings of martyrs and confessors, is not at all out of harmony with the idea of Jesus.

As to miracles, it is fairly evident that Jesus repudiated their apologetic value: "A faithless and perverse generation seek after a sign"; "If they hear not Moses and the prophets, neither will they be persuaded if one rise from the dead"; "Blessed are they that have not seen and yet have believed." These and other texts express the early tradition as to His mind on the subject. But to suppose that he did not believe in miracles, or did not believe that His cures and exorcisms were miraculous, is to suppose a miracle, namely the existence of a nineteenth-century mind in the first century. Doubtless it was not the miracle of our modern apologists and their assailants—a violation of the mechanical order of nature, of a system of rigid uniformities. No such system was dreamt of by the religious mind of those days. Miracles were not supernatural—for nature strictly did not exist—but superhuman. They were the natural works of a superhuman spirit, by which the wonder-worker was "possessed." Even such "possession" was not supernatural, but only unusual. At most miracles were evidence of "possession," but left the good or evil character of the spirit undecided. Hence a moral test had eventually to be applied to discern diabolic from divine miracles. The mere extent of the marvel was of no use. Jesus seems to have discarded the marvel as apologetically worthless, and to have appealed directly to the moral test—to the sign of preaching and prophecy. Allowing, then, for the change that modern science has gradually effected in the conception of miracle, it is plain that the tenacity with which Catholicism defends the miraculous is not out of harmony with the idea of Jesus, and is in no sense a relapse.

One prominent feature of Catholicism we miss in the Christianity of Jesus—namely, any sort of formal theology.

This marriage of revelation with Greek philosophy could only take place on Hellenic soil at a later stage. It was from visions and revelations alone that Jesus drew His knowledge of Heavenly things—from the prophetic and apocalyptic writings and from His own mystical experiences. The casuistry and rationalism of the Scribes and Doctors were profoundly repugnant to Him. What was gathered by such inferences was revealed by "flesh and blood," and not by the Father—vain traditions of men making void the word of God. In form, His revelations were not conceptual and abstract, but imaginative and imaginable. For Him spirit is not the negation but the refinement of matter. It still possesses imaginable content. Later, in her endeavour to philosophise His revelation, the Church had to translate it into conceptual form, and began to draw logical inferences from these concepts and so to build up the whole system of Catholic theology. It is undoubtedly not more easy to recognise the doctrine of Jesus in this form than to recognise nature in the presentments of physical science; and Liberal Protestantism seizes on this difference of form in order to deny that the Church's doctrine was that of Jesus, or that He taught more than an ethic of inward righteousness. As "dogma" usually stands for some defined point of theology, imposed by ecclesiastical authority, it is affirmed confidently that Jesus was not dogmatic. But it is vain to deny that Jesus imposed, with the authority of Divine revelation, and as a matter of life and death, that vision of the transcendental world which the Church has clothed in a theological form. If He did not impose philosophical formulas He imposed the revelation, the imaginative vision, which they formulate. Nor, in theory, does the Church impose the formula except as safeguarding the vision, which it translates into intellectual terms. The authority to which we bow in accepting the formula is not that of theology, but of Christ's revelation as thus formulated. Thus where the difference seems most great it is apparent rather than real.

All said, if the Jesus of Liberal Protestantism is not a pure myth, a shadow of the present darkening the Past, it is only that, having eliminated what was principal in the Gospel, they have retained and segregated what was but secondary and subordinate—the moral element; that which alone can have value for those who have no patience either with the miraculous or the transcendent. For such, Christianity is but the morality of Christ; the Kingdom of Heaven is but the term of moral evolution on earth. God is the law of Righteousness and Jesus the Son of that Law. His life was significant as that of a moral teacher and pattern; His death, as an example of devotion to Righteousness. He has risen in the triumph and spread of His moral teaching, and ascended to God's right hand in the estimation of mankind.

His doctrine is an abiding judgment of the world. His second coming will be at the ideal and unattainable term of man's moral evolution, when all shall be saints and the Kingdom of God realised in its full development on earth. All this is true in a sense, and is ever implied in Christianity. It is an implication that was brought out by a revolt against an excessive transcendentalism under which it had been long stifled. But in vindictively stifling transcendentalism, it has stifled the Jesus of history.

Liberal Protestant Christianity may claim Jesus, if not as the founder, yet as the Great Teacher of its morality. But the morality of Jesus was not the substance of His revelation, any more than was the reason of Jesus. It was not new. It is given by an immanent process to all men in the measure that they use their reason and follow their conscience. The religious idea of Liberal Protestantism is not especially Christian; it is not the "idea" of Jesus. The chasm that Liberal Protestantism finds between Jesus and the earliest Catholicism is of its own creation; the work of prepossession.

In Catholicism we find, amid many accretions no doubt, but in a scarcely altered form, all the leading ideas of Jesus as determined by the steady progress of criticism towards impartial objectivity. Had this criticism any sort of apologetic bias it would certainly not be in favour of Catholicism. Such minor alterations of form as we find are still in harmony with the governing "idea" of the Kingdom of God, and are the result of its protracted delay. Thus the lost stimulus of the immediacy of the End for all was replaced by an insistence on its immediacy for each, on the uncertain certainty of death which was to be followed at once by a private and particular judgment and an entrance of the disembodied soul into Hell or Heaven or Purgatory. The General Judgment was thus reduced in importance and was viewed rather as a solemn pageant of justice already done. The bodily resurrection ceased to be the necessary condition of other-world existence and served only to integrate the joys of Heaven and pains of Hell. The purifying fire of tribulation, through which the just of the generation of Jesus were to pass into Glory, was supplied by Purgatory—a doctrine which is still supported by texts referring to the *Peirasmos* — the fire that is to try every man's work. But plainly these rearrangements of the apocalyptic vision do not seriously affect its substance—the idea of the Church is the idea of Jesus.

X

THE ABIDING VALUE OF THE APOCALYPTIC IDEA

IT is, however, one thing to recognise that, stripped of its theological form, the doctrine of Catholicism is the same as that of Jesus; it is another to contend that, either in its apocalyptic or in its theological form, it can be accepted by the modern mind. If, against Liberal Protestantism, we can vindicate Catholicism as the true Christianity of Christ, do we not seem to bring the Christianity of Christ into peril, and to render the task of the apologist well-nigh impossible? Do we not make it all rest on apocalyptic visions, like those ascribed to Ezechiel, Enoch, John and Baruch?

Christianity, as we have seen, is subordinately and inclusively a religion of righteousness. As, in the progress of thought, faith in the miraculous and transcendent grew weaker, and men's interest was no longer centred on the End by the belief in its imminence, this subordinate value came into prominence. In Protestantism the apocalyptic doctrine has gradually been dropped altogether, or interpreted as symbolic of ethical doctrine. Even in Catholicism emphasis has been laid progressively on the moral element (especially by modern apologists); and symbolism has softened the more repellent features of apocalyptic teachings.

This moralising tendency is no new thing in the Church. It has been long tolerated and encouraged with a view to commend Catholicism on account of its social and political utilities, and to connect religion with the life and interests of a world that shows no sign of disruption. But the Church has felt instinctively that to make Righteousness everything, to treat the Apocalypse as mere moral symbolism, is to introduce a new religion under the old form. She has rightly seen in recent "moralisings" of this kind an encroachment of Liberal Protestantism on Catholic territory. It is an instinct of self-preservation that has roused her to a condemnation of this sort of Modernism. If her rulers are unable to see a distinction between Liberal Catholic and Liberal Protestant Modernism, it is a confusion they share, not only with the unthinking world at large, but with a great number of the Modernists themselves. Although Loisy's *L'Évangile et l'Église* — the classical exposition of Catholic Modernism—was fired straight at the heart of Protestant Modernism, not only the Vatican, but half the world beside, missed its main thesis and saw in it no more than a concession to criticism; and, for the many-headed, that is the sum-total of Modernism. If Catholic Modernists are not yet Protestants they are supposed to be moving towards Protestantism. It is a difference of degree and not of kind. Hence Protestants smile on the movement; and on a good number of its nominal adherents they have a right to smile—on all who accept the Christ of Liberal Protestant criticism, who have not faced the Christ of unbiassed criticism.

It is because Catholic Modernism recognises the identity of the "idea" in Jesus and Catholicism; because it acknowledges that the apocalyptic elements of Christianity are essential and not accidental, the moral elements subordinate and not principal, that, as I have said, it faces the conflict between Christian and modern thought in its purest and acutest form. Were it possible to maintain that the apocalyptic imagery of Jesus was but an ethical parable, taken too grossly in ruder ages and needing only to be restored to its original value, the task would be an easy one. But, since this is impossible, the problem arises as to what value such apocalyptic visions can have for modern religious thought. Compared with this problem, that of the development of present

Catholicism out of the Christianity of Jesus is of slight importance, as soon as we have got rid of the supposed chasm between the Gospel and early Catholicism. This latter was certainly not the dialectical development of theological propositions revealed by Christ. His revelation was imaginative, not conceptual; concrete, not abstract. In substance, and stripped of its theological form, it has lived on in Catholic tradition, especially in the minds of the faithful, whose religious apprehension is imaginative, not conceptual; who have to retranslate theology into vision before it can move their feeling and govern their conduct.

If the revelation of Christ has suffered certain alterations, additions and subtractions, legitimate or illegitimate, it is due to the attempt to harmonise it with changing thought and changing circumstances; to preserve it, not to destroy it. To contend that the Church's *theology* has been always the same is preposterous. Only those who have confounded revelation with its theological presentment could be interested in such a hopeless contention, or could be driven to the expedient of treating potential belief as actual. That confusion dates from the earliest times. But to contend that her *revelation* has been always the same, that the "idea" of Jesus has been faithfully transmitted, is to contend for a plain truth. The difficulty, for us, lies in the fact that this "idea" has been transmitted *too* faithfully, in form and not merely in substance; that this apocalyptic imagery has been given a literal fact-value which our minds have slowly become incapable of accepting, and that we are accordingly tempted to explain it away as a mere parable of the moral life. Yet in this the Church is but true to her Founder, for a Founder He was, when once we abandon the relapse-theory of Liberal Protestantism and recognise the Church as continuous with the "little flock," awaiting and preparing for the Kingdom. For Jesus, what we call His apocalyptic "imagery" was no mere imagery but literal fact. But for us it can be so no longer. We can no longer believe in the little local Heaven above the flat earth, from which Jesus is to appear in the clouds; nor in all the details of the vision governed by this conception. To do so would be to reduce our minds to chaos and scepticism and make us incapable of faith of any sort. Criticism, on the other hand, forbids us to believe that He was making mysteries and puzzles of plain moral truths that He elsewhere expressed plainly, or to deny that He was giving a revelation of the transcendental world of religion. He belonged to the apocalyptics in His religious conceptions, as He did to the prophets in His ethical. Except the identification of Himself with the Son of Man and of the Baptist with Elias, there is nothing original in the form of His revelation. Nowhere does He indicate that these apocalyptic conceptions of the Kingdom were not perfectly familiar to His hearers. He builds on foundations already laid.

What then? Does Christianity rest on the visions of one of a whole school of apocalyptics? Is it worth defending at all? Certainly the great work it has done in the world points to more than this. But may not this be ascribed to moral and prophetic elements, to which its apocalyptic elements gave all the sanctions and reinforcements of religion, thus popularising what else had been a mere school of ethics?

That men believed in the Apocalypse of Jesus as they believed in no other can only be explained by the influence of His extraordinary personality and moral character. No mere wonder-working could have won Him such faith. Wonders were less wonderful then than now; more common; less evidential and unambiguous. Nor did He appeal to them as to apologetic arguments. All they could prove was the presence of a super-human agency, diabolic or divine, in the wonder-worker. Any evidence of the Divine Spirit in Himself was a "miracle," in the sense that the word miracle bore for Jesus and the Scripture. And it was not on physical, but moral, evidence that He relied with such effect. It was because they trusted Him and believed in Him that the people trusted and believed His revelation. His was not merely the power of righteousness, which may repel rather than draw, but the power of love, of deep and universal sympathy with the individual soul; the power of speaking straight to the heart and conscience as God only can speak; of drawing men after Him by a spell they could not understand; of compelling them by an authority which they felt but could not explain. They could not help trusting and believing in Him absolutely: "Whither thou goest I will go: thy people shall be my people, and thy God my God: Where thou diest will I die and there will I be buried."

There is thus some basis for the tendency of a rationalising and moralising Christianity to find the revelation of Jesus in His moral personality and character, in His concrete exemplification or embodiment of the so-called new Righteousness; to attach as little importance to His religious imagery as to His scientific or historic ideas—which were those of His time. But it may be questioned whether a great deal of the faith that He commanded was not the fruit of His faith in Himself as the Son of Man, the vicegerent and plenipotentiary of God; whether the authority with which He spoke and convinced was not inspired by His Messianic secret. Did He speak merely as a prophet, in the name of morals and with the authority of conscience and not also in the name of the Son of Man? Had the sense of the supernatural nothing to do with His mysterious power over men? the sense that God was with Him and He with God, in some undefinable manner? If it had, we must then allow that His power flowed from His sense of being, not merely moral but superhuman; that His apocalyptic idea entered into and formed His personality; that, without it, His influence is not adequately explained.

And I think this may be extended to the moral influence of Christianity in the world. Had it been merely moral, and not also transcendental, could it have done what it has done? When it is purged of all transcendental meaning and value, will Righteousness be able to hold its own?

Can we then bow down before the moral pre-eminence of such a personality and, at the same time, regard its religious ideas as illusory and negligible? However different in the abstract, morality and religion are fused together in the living spirit. Moral purity of heart purifies our intuition of the Divine. Is it credible that the purest of all hearts should not have seen God; that it should have been the prey to a sort of religious delirium? Is it possible to trust the moral, and distrust the religious, intuitions of Jesus?

Must we not rather think that, however untenable in form, the "idea" of Jesus and of Catholic Christianity stands for a conception of religion answering, in elevation and dignity, to the morality with which it was fused in His mind? that the Heaven to which this righteousness was subordinate cannot have been that of a lower plane of spirituality?

We spoke, some time back, of the "religious idea" as governing man's need to adjust himself to the invisible world which lies beyond the range of his sensible experience. The religion of the individual consists of certain images (or even concepts) of that world and its relation to man; of certain feelings, emotions and desires, determined by those images; of certain observances and actions adjusting man to that life beyond. As such, religion has to do with the transcendent—with the other world, not with this. Only when man has risen to the idea of a moral God, and of Righteousness as the will and service of God, are morality and religion closely connected. Of itself morality is occupied with our duty towards our neighbour. Not till we get to an ethical religion is our duty towards our neighbour seen as also a duty towards

God, as the highest form of worship. It takes on a transcendent or religious aspect. But religion, as such, deals entirely with the transcendent. Its "idea" unfolds itself and comes into clearer consciousness in an infinity of directions and degrees, dependent on its mental, moral and social environment—on the materials out of which it has to weave an embodiment for itself. But, from the nature of the case, its presentment of the transcendent order, and of the present order in its relation to the transcendent, can never be more than symbolic. And this, not because the transcendent is absolutely unknowable in such sort that we have no term of comparison at all. To such a world there could be no need to relate ourselves. It could not touch us, nor we it. For us it were simply non-existent. But whatever little fraction of experience mankind possesses can never be more than a symbol of the totality of possible experience that lies beyond. A man is not absolutely unknowable for a mouse, but the mouse's knowledge of him can only be in terms of mouse-life. Man's highest God will be man writ large. By no process of abstraction or magnification or subtraction can the human be purged out of our concepts of God, or of anything else above or below us.

Yet our symbolisms of the transcendent vary in value and truth. Like scientific hypotheses, those are the best that bring our life most fully into harmony with the world they symbolise; which best satisfy our needs, deepen our experiences, answer to our faith. It is not too much to say that mankind feels its way to these symbols and hypotheses as a blind man feels his way to the fire. Man is uneasy; he seeks rest for his soul; he gropes about and follows the direction that is confirmed by his religious and moral experience. That he gives absolute, instead of hypothetic, value to his constructions is perhaps a misfortune, in that it leads him to do violence to later and fuller experience. But so far as a hypothesis gives a correct anticipation and control of experience it is true.

To pretend that Jesus regarded His apocalyptic portrayal of the transcendent as symbolic is to pretend that His mind belonged to the nineteenth century. It was for Him no more a figure of the transcendent than it was a figure of the moral life. And the same must be said of Catholicism, which has been true, not merely to the religious "idea" of Jesus, but to its very form. That form, as we have said, has lost all literal truth for us. It can no longer produce in us the fruits it produced in simpler ages. It belonged to a world that was but six thousand years old and had no future before it; to a petty universe of which that world was the sole and central preoccupation. It had not even behind it the prestige of the whole religious history of Israel. The apocalyptic literature was an exotic, a late introduction into the religion of Israel. And yet the fact remains that it was in the forms of apocalyptic thought that the religious "idea" of Jesus embodied itself, and exercised the most potent religious influence that the world has yet known. It is idle to pretend that His influence has been purely ethical. He has satisfied, not only the moral, but the mystical, needs of millions for centuries, and His moral influence has been largely dependent on His mystical influence. We cannot even say that we owe the apocalyptic form to Jesus, that it was the creation of His spirit. He found it to hand. It was the religious language of His surroundings. He had not first to invent and teach a new language before He could communicate with His people. He took the existing language as the medium, not only of His speech, but of His thought. His own place in the apocalyptic scheme was the substance of His personal revelation. For the rest He adopted the revelations of others.

It would seem, then, an obvious duty to abandon the apocalyptic form and retain what it stands for and embodies. This would be easy if it stood for ethical principles. The symbolic presentment of what can be expressed properly is inexcusable. But the transcendental can never be expressed properly. Translated into the terms of our present philosophy, the "idea" of Jesus remains symbolic. To whatever degree we dematerialise our symbols of the spiritual, material they must remain. Our own symbolism would be as unacceptable for a later age as the apocalyptic symbolism is for us. The only remedy lies in a frank admission of the principle of symbolism. With this admission we have no need to abolish the Apocalypse, which, as the form in which Jesus embodied His religious "idea," is classical and normative for all subsequent interpretations of the same. In the long series of translations the original sense may be easily perverted if the original text be lost. What each age has to do is to interpret the apocalyptic symbolism into terms of its own symbolism.

How, then, should we express the religious "idea" of Jesus in our own age? What, for us, are the values underlying the apocalyptic revelation? How, had He belonged to our own day, and had His mind been stored with our historical, scientific, philosophical, moral and religious beliefs, would His religious "idea" have clothed itself, and remained the same "idea"?

It is "the same," in so far as it produces the same level and degree of spiritual life and experience. The same relation may be described, the same direction given, in endless ways. The truth of all these ways is the same if they yield the same control over experience. To say they are but symbolic of the transcendent is not agnosticism; since symbols may be representative. Nor is it pure pragmatism, since the degree of their practical utility is just that of their correspondence to reality. Were nature not in some way like a mechanism, the determinist hypothesis of science would be fruitless. Because the likeness is imperfect, the fruitfulness is imperfect. Taken as the whole account of nature, the hypothesis starves the better half of man's soul.

Any construction of the transcendent that yields the same fruits as the apocalyptic construction is true to the "idea" of Jesus. We have not to compare symbol with symbol, or theology with theology, or to show that one can be deduced from the other. We have to compare life with life; feeling with feeling; action with action.

XI

THE TRUTH-VALUE OF VISIONS

THE word "visionary" is too widely associated with illusion not to inspire a profound distrust. In an age of psychological ignorance the easy credit accorded to the visionary was open to great abuse. Even fairly truthful men are not so scrupulously accurate about their statements when these cannot be checked. When few travelled, a "traveller's tale" meant a fiction, and a sailor's "yarn" was not taken seriously. Authority is always abused in the absence of safeguards, and the authority of knowledge follows the rule. In days of larger credit and credulity an impostor could pretend to visions, and the true visionary re-edit his visions to suit his desires.

Another element of illusion was the "objectification" of visions. Obvious as it is to us, the distinction between subjective and objective appearances is a slow acquisition of mental development, and by no means completed even yet. It is not one of "vividness"; for our dreams, and even our waking imaginations, are often more vivid than our true perceptions. Both systems of appearances are, in some sense, our own creation. But the latter is common to all men, and is determined by some principle of regular sequence and grouping which evades our control. This is a difference that can only be learnt gradually by experience. The range of the objective grows with human experience: just as life teaches us that many things, which, as children, we thought peculiar to ourselves, belong to human nature as such. An appearance is illusory only when we place it in the wrong series and are led into consequent errors of anticipation—as when we mistake our dreams for facts and calculate accordingly. An accidental vividness of imagination and weakness of perception and vitality may project a dream into space and history; and only by its irrelevance to the objective series can the hallucination be detected. A vision is a hallucination so far as it seems to belong to, and come from, the objective series, and this because it is not seen to belong to the subjective series. This error of psychological interpretation has something to do with the distrust of visionaries in these days.

Connected with this error of "objectification" is the tendency to attach a literal, and not merely a symbolic, value to their content, when they are accepted as revelations of transcendental realities;

and to be amazed, for example, at the divergencies between the Sacred Passion according to S. Bridget and the same according to Sister Catherine Emmerich.

All this does not exclude the fact that visions are a perfectly normal phenomenon of the human mind, and possess a certain sort of truth-value. Every movement of consciousness is from the implicit and vague to the explicit and distinct. It unfolds itself in more definite feelings, impulses, images and even concepts. When the movement is sudden and strong, the image is sudden and strong. Its abruptness and force seem to detach it from the subjective series and so to throw it into the objective. Yet this accidental illusion in no way affects the value of its content, except so far as, to those who are under sway of the illusion, it may seem to give this content a divine and miraculous authority. It may, however, have divine authority on a different title—namely, so far as the inward movement from which it springs is divine.

The sense of an absolute opposed to his relativity, an infinite to his finitude, a permanent to his evanescence, an actual to his potentiality, a repose to his restlessness, is the groundwork and canvas on which man's rational life is broidered. Because it is permanent, like the burden of a melody, it is not an object of distinct advertence any more than the air we breathe or the space we move in. We adjust ourselves to it in many ways as unconsciously as we do to the laws of life or thought. It needs some effort of reflection to separate the religious from the other factors of our spirit-life; to study and develop them apart. We do not need to prove religion to men, but to show them that they are religious. That religion which we "prove" is not the substance, but a particular form and interpretation of religious experience—not the divine, but some particular image, symbol or conception of the divine. What we experience (be our creed or non-creed what it may) is a Power that makes for Righteousness, i.e. that subjects us to an universal, super-individual, super-social end, of which we have no distinct conception, and which we can only figure to ourselves in symbols and images, whether spontaneously or by a deliberate effort of thought. That we can feel and suffer from our relativity, finitude and evanescence, means an under-consciousness of an Absolute, Infinite and Unchanging, that we must for ever try to express in our thought and action as in terms of another order of being. The energy, constancy and sincerity with which we pursue this task is the measure of our spiritual life. Only when we are so perfect as to pursue it without let or hindrance, shall we have found such rest as the finite spirit is capable of.

This need of harmony between himself and the transcendent is, as we have said, the essence of the religious "idea." Man's need of righteousness is but subordinate to it. His æsthetic and intellectual needs belong to it just as truly. In all three he seeks the unattainable absolute and is ever dissatisfied with his best attainments.

When it is objected that inward experience does not give us God, this must be admitted if by "God" we mean some particular image, symbol or idea. Such symbols are always the spontaneous or deliberate representation of the transcendent cause or source of the experience. They are "mysteries," objects of faith. But to object that the cause or source is not revealed to us in the experience is to mistake the very idea of a real cause. In the modern scientific sense a cause is merely a group of antecedent phenomena. And God is not such a cause. But a real cause or agent is only revealable in, through and with its effects or appearances—as affecting us in some way. In this sense God can be revealed to us in experiences, just as our fellow-men are. He is an object of that faith which enters into our simplest judgments—the faith by which we believe in an objective world, or in minds other than our own. I do not find my fellow-man *in*, but *through* my experience; by a work of spontaneous interpretation. If my idea of him be not merely a symbol, it is because I have an adequate measure of him in myself; whereas God does not belong to the world of external sense, nor is His nature expressible properly in terms of my own. The first instinct of thought is to treat everything as another self—to exalt what is below us, to abase what is above us, to that level. Differentiation is the slow work of experience and reflection—a work which can never be complete. Of the absolutely diverse we could have no conception, no desire, no need. Our first notion of God, naturally, is human. We gradually dehumanise it to the idea of an infinite human spirit. If we go further and cancel the last feature of humanity, we are left with something absolute, unrelated and simply diverse, that does not exist for us. We cannot adjust our life to what does not touch us or enter into our environment. Only so far as the absolute is also immanent, and mingles with the world's process, can religion have an object.

This process of man's self-adjustment to the immanent-transcendent implies action and reaction. The Divine is no dead and passive environment, but a living, active, social environment. God gives and man receives; God leads and man follows. By his inward experiences of felt harmony or discord with the transcendent, man can test the value of his religious notions and of the conduct they dictate. It is in those experiences that God guides him directly. There is no other language between the soul and God. The spontaneous or deliberate symbols, in which those experiences take mental shape, serve directly to embody and retain the experience; to make it in some way communicable; to fix the direction of life, the tone of feeling, suggested by it. Like the hypotheses of science, they serve to co-ordinate and control phenomena, and in the measure that they do so they are founded in and represent reality—albeit symbolically. When we realise how purely symbolic even our best and most fruitful scientific hypotheses must be, on how infinitesimal an experience of the whole they are founded, we can see that revelation involves no violation of the usual processes of thought, nor calls for any sort of special faculty.

Thus there is no more reason for an indiscriminate contempt of revelation than for a like contempt of other means of knowledge—and we cannot exclude from the realm of "knowledge" the record and classification of any department of experience, however incapable of exact expression. Tradition, induction, deduction, observation can be, and have been, as widely abused. Their laws and criteria have been slowly determined. Empirical gave place to scientific medicine, as soon as analysis and induction had established the true chains of antecedents and consequents. Religion is still in the empirical stage in many respects. It has no clear method of distinguishing sham from reality and of justifying the values it has learnt by experience.

As things are, the only test of revelation is the test of life—not merely of moral, but of spiritual, fruitfulness in the deepest sense. It must at once satisfy and intensify man's mystical and moral need. It must bring the transcendent nearer to his thoughts, feelings and desires. It must deepen his consciousness of union with God. This, as we have said, was the "evidence" to which Jesus appealed in proof of His "possession" by God's spirit—the evidence of His control over man's mystical life. His revelation was the secret of that control; of the fire that He was and the fire that He came to spread. Such, too, is the evidence of Christianity as a personal religion—its power over souls that are already Christian in sympathy and capacity; the soul-compelling power of the spirit of Christ. Any other "sign," be it miracle or argument, will appeal only to the faithless and perverse. It may puzzle them, but it will never convince them; it may convert them to the Church, but it cannot convert them to God; it may change their theology—it cannot change their hearts.

XII

THE APOCALYPTIC VISION OF CHRIST

(a) THE TRANSCENDENCY OF THE KINGDOM

HOW, then, must we, here and now, understand the apocalyptic and transcendental revelation of Jesus, so as to shape our spiritual life, feeling and action in harmony with His? How must we re-embody the same "idea" if it is to live for us?

First of all we must recognise that morality is not our highest life, but only a particular manifestation of it under certain contingencies. So far as morality is the will of God, it unites man dynamically with God. But it is not conscious union until the moral experience receives a religious and transcendent interpretation—until the absolute peremptoriness of right over all personal, social or racial interests is more or less recognised as that of a Will, whose object is universal and eternal Right, and in subjection to which our wills find their true life and expansion. It is just the conscious aiming at this union with the transcendent, through the moral life, that raises morality to religion—to a conscious self-adjustment to the realities of the transcendent world.

But besides the "ought" of conduct there is the "ought" of thinking and the "ought" of feeling—the duty of a complete and ever completer harmony of the whole spirit—mind, heart, will and action—with what we necessarily conceive as a perfect Spirit, without limitations. However obscure and rudimentary, the need of this harmony becomes explicit in the love and exercise of any sort of rightness—moral, intellectual or æsthetic—for its own sake. Man's need of harmony with the Divine is as natural as his need of bread. If this harmony be an ideal or end "in process of becoming," it supposes, as its other term, the Divine, as something actual and given. The moral life, therefore, is potentially, and may become actually, religious; it may help to satisfy man's mystical need of conscious union with the transcendent; but it can never be the whole of religion, and need not be religious at all.

To maintain that religion is man's highest life, it seems to me that we must deny a vital continuity between the lowest and the highest forms of religion. The former, I cannot but think, belong strictly to the category of magic, or rudimentary natural science. In the interests of his non-moral life the savage desires to control the invisible powers that govern the sequence of phenomena—powers usually conceived as personal. His gods are as much part of the order of nature as are our hypothetical "forces" and "laws." He wants to be friends with his god, because it is the best way to control that "force" to his own temporal advantage. But union with his god is not, for the savage, an end in itself, or the satisfaction of a spiritual need. Only so far as he has some rudimentary moral sense, some love of rightness for its own sake, does he possess a sort of virtual religion. Not till he images God as a moral being, and recognises morality as the Will of the Highest, as the sovereign and universal Good; not till union with such a God becomes for him an end in itself, and his own ultimate perfection, does he pass from magic to religion.

The continuity of religion is one of form and expression, rather than of substance and content. A new god takes over the regalia of the old—his names, his temples, his rites. We thus find the surviving forms of the earliest religion in the latest, and this in virtue of the laws of the human mind. But there is no continuity of substance between magical and moral religion. The latter is the development of a non-religious morality that co-existed side by side with non-moral magical religion, till the day when morality took over the regalia of religion. The religion of magic, being wholly subordinate to man's physical and temporal interests, belongs to man's lower and individual life. As such it is far beneath his moral and universal life in dignity. But the religion that grew out of morality is something higher and fuller than morality. "Higher and fuller," because, with it, man becomes consciously and actively the organ of an universal and eternal life, the instrument of an universal and eternal end; because, with it, his physical selfhood is transcended and subordinated to his spiritual selfhood or personality. Religion deepens and is deepened by his profound and divine discontent. With every development of his spiritual faculties his rebellion against his own relativity, finitude and evanescence increases. He feels that no mere extension of his individual life could satisfy him; nay, by experience he learns that such extensions leave him less, and not more, content. He wants to pass εἰς ἄλλο γένος; and the want implies an unsatisfied capacity for so doing. There is that in him which nothing can satisfy but some sort of union with and appropriation of the infinite and eternal. In the measure that he tries to live widely, deeply and nobly he is bound to become a pessimist. If optimism is usually associated with the youth and pessimism with the age of persons or peoples, it is because pessimism is the verdict of experience. Whether in himself, or in the world, if a man has ideals for both, he is bound to find not only failure, but an iron law of inevitable failure, of progress thwarted and frustrated even by its multiplicity and fecundity—its waves dashed to futile spray by their very force and volume. From such a world and such a life he must seek refuge in an abiding City, that hath foundations whose builder and maker is God. Only so established can he have patience, courage and hope to join in the struggle between the Divine Will and the forces of evil in himself and in the world, not asking to see the meaning and issue of it all, but working blindly along with Him Who sees.

Born of a felt contrast between the actual and man's wakening spiritual ideals, combined with the gradual recognition of the schism as inevitable and unconquerable, this pessimism is the presupposition of that optimism of blind faith by which it is overcome. They are two stages in the same process of spiritual growth—a process that we find arrested in Buddhism. If it be not arrested, it is strangely perverted in what may be called Modern Christianity, whose optimism is begotten of faith in this world, not of faith in the other; whose courage and hope is maintained by the belief that the schism between the ideal and the actual will eventually be healed through an inherent *vis medicatrix Naturæ*, that the Kingdom of God is the natural term of a process of moral and social development.

Nothing is more evident than that Jesus had no such faith or hope. The revelation of the apocalyptic Kingdom of Heaven was a Gospel or Good News for those who despaired of the world. It supplanted and reinterpreted, in a transcendental sense, the earlier prophetic Gospel of the temporal triumph of Israel and the reign of moral and legal righteousness on earth—a Gospel that experience of the law of failure had discredited. The mere fact that he expected the Kingdom tomorrow proves that the faith and hope of Jesus was not in progress or evolution. What sort of Gospel had it been for the poor, the sorrowful, the persecuted, the oppressed, to know that, not they, but their class, would be relieved in some remote age by the advance of civilisation and morality? Had it not been to satisfy their hunger with stones and their thirst with gall and vinegar?

The verdict of the deeper spiritual intuition on this life is always pessimistic, and it is a verdict that is only confirmed by experience and reflection. It is evident that there are vital and progressive forces at work everywhere, but it is equally plain that there are destructive forces, that life is strangled by its own fertility, that it is faced by the insoluble problem of finding room for its expansion in every direction, that the utmost its ingenuity can do is to defer the inevitable day of defeat and to prolong its periods of uninterrupted progress. The world is the arena of a conflict between a multitude of irreconcilable ends. The belief that they are ordained to an eventual harmony, however useful as a stimulus to combat, falls to pieces on closer inspection, which reveals an inherent fault or rift in nature. All life is under the sway of sad mortality.

To-day we are so enamoured of our scientific and material progress that we have no eyes for our many decadences, even though we are face to face with social and moral chaos. We believe, with childish simplicity, that we are making straight for the millennium. We forget that every new comfort is a new necessity, a new source of discontent and unhappiness, and leaves the relative proportion of happiness and misery unaffected. Thrust out at one place the tide of sorrow breaks in at another: *expellas furca tamen usque recurret.* If medicine cures diseases, it enables the diseased to increase and multiply and re-establish the average of unhealthiness. Shall progress ever wipe away the tears from all eyes? Shall it ever extinguish love and pride and ambition and all the griefs attendant in their train? Is it enough to give a man bread for his belly and instruction for his brain? Prolong life as it will, can progress conquer death, with its terrors for the dying, its tears for the surviving? Can it ever control the earthquake, the tempest, the lightning, the cruelties of a nature indifferent to the lot of man? And even, given the attainment of its facile dreams, can progress postpone the day when mankind shall be blotted off the face of a universe, that will go its way as though he had never been?

The root of this fallacy of progress is the uncriticised and indefensible assumption that the race and the whole world, like the individual organism, are inherently predetermined to pass through a series of stages ending in a definite final perfection. That sort of development belongs only to the individual organism. That of the species or race is determined casually from without, not predetermined from within. It is a result rather than an end—the result of conflict with accidental and incalculable difficulties; a result that no insight into present conditions could predict. Progress makes for no preordained goal. The race is predetermined to live on indefinitely, and to do so it must learn to overcome the obstacles it encounters in its expansion. Its course is no more planned than the course of a river. It runs on and expands, because it must, and how it must. Different obstructions would have called forth different arts, skills and inventions; so the present course of progress is only one out of thousands that might have been. Altogether the dream of a possible earthly paradise, in which the travail of nature is to culminate, has no other basis than a false analogy between progress and organic life. So far as the moral struggle is explained and justified by this imaginary and impossible end, it is a mere beating of the air. Only an eternal and universal end can explain the imperative and absolute character of Right; and humanity is neither eternal nor universal. The Right must be worth doing even were the world to vanish the next moment. But that universal and eternal end is necessarily unimaginable for the human mind, limited to a brief moment of duration and to a mere point in the range of possible experience. Yet we are fain to give some figure, some content, to the idea of that universal end; and prone to forget the symbolic character of that figure. We have none better, perhaps, than the image of a perfectly happy world, produced by a steady process of moral development. Only when we realise the inherent contradictions of such a concept, do we see that we have mistaken a symbol for reality.

The apocalyptic Kingdom of Heaven is not

more of a dream and unreality; but there is far less danger of our overlooking its symbolic character. It is presented to us as an object of faith and revelation, not as an object of rational foresight. It is a bliss given by God, not wrought out by man; a bliss into which all may enter and not merely a favoured and final generation in a remote future. It is the fruit and reward of the moral life, but is a supermoral life—the continuation of that divine and spiritual life which, under present contingencies, manifests itself principally in morality, in rightness of conduct, though also in rightness of thought and feeling and, above all, in religion and conscious union with God. But there the contingencies, that now call for the moral struggle with all its pain and suffering, shall be done away. It is the rest that remains for the people of God. Here there is for the just a foretaste of that rest in the midst of their labours and tribulations; for to have God is to have rest. But till they have Him fully and undividedly their rest is broken with restlessness. Rest is the motive and end of the soul's struggle with the waves that would bear it from the Rock to which it clings. So closely are the struggle and the rest associated in our experience that the saints seem almost to love the struggle for its own sake, and to shrink from the idea of an eternal and unbroken rest.

Yet the Peirasmos, or Temptation, is none the less an evil. Christ did not say "Lead us" but "Lead us *not* into the Peirasmos." But action is not opposed to rest. And union with God is union with the Divine Life and Action, with the undisturbed centre of the cyclone.

In the tangle and contradiction of the world of our present experience goodness, beauty, truth and happiness are at discord. Against this discord our whole spiritual nature revolts. It strives, and is bound to strive, to overcome this violation of order. And yet it can do no more than mitigate an inevitable and perpetual evil. No conceivable degree of progress could ever satisfy this deepest demand of our nature. And even if it could, the vision would not be for our eyes but for those of a final, and immeasurably distant, generation. The whole idea of the subordination of past and present humanity to the interests of a remote futurity, as means to an end, belongs to the false comparison of the life of the race to that of an individual organism. We live for our own sakes and not for a posterity that never comes. We have equal rights with any generation of the future. The truth is that neither we nor they shall find goodness, happiness, truth and beauty united in this life.

As man progresses mentally and morally, he is

likely to find the discord increased rather than diminished. The deepest demand of his nature is the last to rise to the surface of explicit consciousness. As he grows spiritually, he asks more and not less, and seems to receive less and not more. And to this his revolt against earlier and inadequate expressions of the religious idea is due in a great measure. Taken literally, and not symbolically, they do not meet his need. And as long as he demands to picture to himself distinctly the term and satisfaction of that need he is doomed to doubt, for his picturings will necessarily be drawn from the world of his present experience. Not till he resigns the desire to see what is hopelessly beyond the range of his present vision, is his faith pure and unshaken. Faith believes that this need relates to another order of experience; that the present order serves only to evoke, exercise and strengthen it, but can never satisfy it. This implies that, in his deepest being, man belongs already to that other order. He has a power, whose meaning and purpose are hid from him through lack of a proper object for their exercise. A cage-born bird, he wonders what his wings are for. He tries to make a heaven out of earth, as it were ropes out of sand. He was made for something else—he does not know what. Like the domesticated beaver he builds his dams across the floor; he cannot tell why. Not till he is in his native river will he understand his restless instinct; and the river is beyond all his present experience and imagination—a missing link in his mind.

As far, then, as the apocalyptic Kingdom of Heaven stands for an order of transcendental experience, in which sorrow, pain, temptation and sin shall be done away; in which the moral struggle shall be explained, justified and brought to eternal rest; in which the spiritual discords of our present experience shall be harmonised; in which man shall understand the meaning of those deepest needs, to which the present order is educational and preparatory; as far as it stands for that which is the gift of God and not the result of development—so far it seems to me to express symbolically the religious idea, brought to an advanced stage of explicitness. Treated as symbolic, not of transcendent life but of man's moral experience in the present life, it ceases to be that Gospel or Good News which alone makes life bearable for those to whom instinct, experience and reflection have revealed the shallowness of the Gospel of progress and the promise of salvation by development. Doubtless these despairing idealists are a minority, but they are what all men tend to become in the measure of their spiritual development. And, after all, five hundred millions of Buddhists share their pessimism, though not the hope that alleviates it. None should be so ripe for the Gospel; though not for the Gospel of Liberal Protestantism, with its bland faith and hope in the present order, its refusal to face the incurable tragedy of human life—a tragedy that grows deeper as man rises from the hand-to-mouth simplicity of mere animal existence, extends his knowledge and control of experience and wakes ever more fully to the sense of his insatiable exigencies. The more truly he is man, the more truly he is miserable. If he have no hope beyond earth, he can do no better than contract his desires to the point of extinction, unless his humanity be sufficiently latent to let him live like a gnat in a sunbeam.

(b) IMMORTALITY

The apocalyptic Kingdom of Heaven assumes a life after death, a continuation, expansion and revelation of the life of the spirit as lived even now by the righteous. The belief in immortality is not essential to magical religions, in which gods are dealt with as powers of nature, to be controlled in man's temporal interests; in which their friendship is not an end, but a utility. Thus the early religion of Israel had no hope beyond the grave. In many such primitive peoples there prevails a belief in some dreamland, whither the soul (a shade of the body) wanders in sleep or after death; but this belief is not necessarily religious. At most there is a hope that, so far as this life is continued at low pressure in Hades, the gods who have been propitious here may extend their favour to that land of shadows and memories. But it is a poorer, not a richer and fuller, existence than the present. The least upon earth is better than the greatest under the earth; whereas, for Christianity, the greatest born of woman is less than the least in the Kingdom of Heaven. Between these conceptions of immortality there is no continuity of substance, but only of form. The terms and images of the earlier belief have, to some extent, been appropriated by the later, somewhat to the prejudice of truth.

As true spiritual religion is a development, not of magical religion, but of the moral life, so also belief in spiritual immortality has not sprung from belief in ghosts and shades, but from the same root as spiritual religion. Whether recognised or only implicit, it is a postulate of the moral life. I cannot desire what is not in some sense my own good, my own end; and yet I desire the right, i.e. what is good irrespectively of my own individual and temporal interests and of those of all humanity. *Fiat justitia ruat cœlum*, is the dictate of the moral conscience. Everything temporal must be sacrificed to this absolute and imperative good. When we say that righteousness must be disinterested, we only exclude these temporal interests. Were it not our own interest in some sense, it could not be an object of will at all. It is therefore my own interest, because I am a spiritual, super-temporal and super-individual being; because, as such, my interest is identified with that of an eternal and universal Will. Hence I feel that what matters for me absolutely, matters for me eternally. This I could not feel were I convinced that, when the human race is wiped out of the physical world, it will not matter whether I have lived well or ill.

Men have lived, and do live, moral lives without any implicit recognition of such a postulate. But even if they explicitly deny it with their reason, it is affirmed by their instinct and their conduct. Connecting the doctrine of immortality, in its popular materialistic setting, with a hope of temporal reward, deferred in this life, to be bestowed in a continuation of a similar order of experience, they rightly feel it a nobler thing to love justice for its own sake, and not for the sake of a lower happiness. To say that this love or satisfaction is, in itself, a reward, and that such men are, therefore, self-interested, is a mere quibble. The self-interest that spoils moral purity is the interest of the individual organic self, not that of the universal and spiritual self; it is that which belongs to our consciousness of being separate from all, not to our consciousness of being identified with all. The desire of an immortality, which means the persistence and expansion of that very love of justice, cannot sully the purity of the heart. It is objectively inseparable from such a love, which implies the desire to be with God, and therefore to be with Him always.

As we have said before, the transcendent and universal end, that justifies the imperative and absolute character of Right, is hopelessly unimaginable for us who command but a moment of duration and a point of immensity. We can only present it to ourselves under symbols drawn from our present experience. So, too, our symbols of the life immortal, drawn largely from animistic and magical religions, imperil the spirituality of the belief, and propose it to us as an object of vision rather than of faith. And this not less but more, when, discarding the symbols of the imagination, we have recourse to those of the understanding and try to conceive the when, where and how of life eternal.

Philosophy can neither give us that faith nor take it from us. It is given us in the moral instinct, which we can no more repress than we can repress our belief in personalities other than our own. The sceptic who denies it may be unanswerable, but he convinces neither us nor himself. His very denial implies his sense that truth matters absolutely and eternally. All that philosophy can do is to criticise our attempted statements and interpretation of the instinct. These, being necessarily in terms of temporal experience and life, may conflict with that experience if they be taken as more than symbolic of the transcendent and unimaginable. Such criticism is as irrelevant as if it were applied to the apocalyptic Kingdom of Heaven. We only know our spiritual life in relation to, and in conflict with, certain conditions—conditions which hinder and limit its full manifestations: in which it can never realise itself and come to rest. Any ideal condition we can *imagine* must be of the same kind in some new and inherently impossible arrangement, e.g. a world of perfectly moral men in which morality would be *ipso facto* impossible; a world of goods without their essentially correlative evils; in short, a world of hills without valleys. Yet these imaginings are the necessary symbol of that unimaginable reality which answers to our spiritual need—they are "mysteries"; objects of faith; signs of an unseen.

And what can any philosophy do for or against our faith in that unseen? Can it ever even tell us what matter is, or what spirit is; whether they be two, or but two aspects of one; and, if two, how they are related? Are not all our relations, such as twoness and oneness, borrowed from the spatial and temporal, and therefore senseless outside that realm? Can it even tell us what we ourselves, makers of space and time, are? Is the mystery of the Trinity more full of insoluble contradictions than that of our own selfhood? I may know everything more easily than what "I" the knower am. Can I know my thinking self apart from the objects of my thought of which that self is co-factor? When I try to think of it I at once distort it into some object—usually my body—which is but its symbol. And if I cannot know the relation between the perceived object, that I call my body, and myself, for which it is object, am I likely to know the relation between myself and God? When I conceive it as identity or diversity my eyes are full of dust, my thought is charged with materialism. I am dealing with a symbol of myself and with a symbol of God, as with two spatial objects. Only my spiritual experience, my moral exigencies, compel me to think and act alternately as though there were at once identity and diversity. Of the transcendent basis of that instinct I know (Newman would say) as much as any man, and that is absolutely nothing. All I know is a hunger that I can mitigate with dust and bran, but whose plenary satisfaction I cannot imagine, however I try to heap incompatibles together.

The desire for this spiritual immortality is, then, totally distinct from that desire for a perpetuation of the present life which fits in with magical religion, and has for its object, not eternal life but an endless prolongation of temporal life. To a great extent these desires vary inversely. To the young, vigorous, fortunate and inexperienced, the thought of death is as intolerable as the thought of sleep to an active man in the bright freshness of morning. But night brings a change and a desire for rest and unconsciousness. Men live their fill and want no more of this life. Its endless prolongation would be hell. But in the measure that they have seen through the illusions of this outward experience they are more likely to wake to the need of another sort of experience. As the eternal life that is in them asserts itself, the thought of its extinction grows more intolerable and the faith in its perpetuity more imperative. The immortality that spiritualism strives to establish experimentally is simply a prolongation of this temporal life, in the absence of that environment out of which it is utterly meaningless and positively inconceivable. Moreover the quest is vitiated by the animistic conception of the soul, as a sprite that enters the body at birth and leaves it at death—i.e. as something spatial and material, a shade of the body. Of spiritual immortality there is not, and cannot be, any sort of experimental or philosophical demonstration. Like our belief in God or in other personalities, it is a matter of faith; an inevitable, though not logically inevitable, interpretation of spiritual experience.

That this faith comes late in the history of religion is no more surprising than that a purer morality and more spiritual religion should be similarly delayed. It is none the less natural, for man's nature unfolds its potentialities gradually, the deepest and most fundamental being the last to appear.

In early Israel the future life was but the sad ghost of the present—"They that go down into the pit cannot hope for Thy truth: The living, the living, he shall praise Thee." Earth, and not Sheôl, was the place of divine rewards and punishments. The people were one corporate personality, in which all were responsible for the actions of each, and were punished or rewarded accordingly.

Before God, Israel was everything; the individual only a member of Israel. And Israel had the immortal duration of a people, wherein to suffer or gain by the deeds of its members. Not till the personality and sole responsibility of the individual came to be recognised, did the problem of Job and *Ecclesiastes* become pressing. Experience showed that God did not serve individual men in this life according to their works. As yet there was no thought of an adjustment in a future life. In Sheôl all were equal in their misery and darkness. The schism between duty and happiness was viewed as permanent—as a mystery to be accepted in silence and faith, or else as a justification of moral and religious scepticism. Later came the prophetic hope of the triumph of Israel, captive and oppressed, over the Gentiles, and a reign of moral and legal righteousness on earth. Here, then, was the solution. The just of past ages would rise in their bodies and enter into that Kingdom, while the wicked would be left in the gloom and misery of Sheôl.

In all this we must recognise the gradual coming to consciousness of the moral sense with its postulate of immortality; its tendency to shape the world of its desire out of the world that is, by some impossible rearrangement of life and history. The prophet's dream was an attempted interpretation of the exigencies of his moral and religious instinct; a seeking for a transcendent reality in the lower plane of the present. And the stronger and deeper his instinct, so much the bolder and grander his vision and so much the closer does its fulfilment appear. The belief that its ideals must be fulfilled, and fulfilled soon, is inseparable from spiritual intensity and ardour. Thus prophet after prophet proclaimed the triumph of Israel on the morrow, and time after time it proved that the end was not yet; that the vision was but symbolic of a reality beyond vision and beyond time.

As hope in the coming theocracy failed under the repeated blows of disappointment, a new generation of prophets left the world to its fate, as incurably given over to the powers of evil. Nothing was to be hoped for from the course of events; they believed no longer in any organised plan that was working mysteriously, in spite of its seeming crookedness, for the triumph of Israel. For the later apocalyptic seers the kingdoms of this world had been usurped by Satan. They could be redeemed to God only through the conquest of Satan and his angels by the Son of Man and His angels. God's Kingdom was not to grow out of the earth but to descend upon it from above, ready-made and complete.

This conception marks a further advance in the

interpretation of man's spiritual exigencies. It recognises that they cannot be satisfied in the natural order, but only in a transcendent world and by an entirely new kind of experience. No doubt that transcendent experience is figured in terms of our present experience. It cannot be otherwise if we figure it at all; and yet the unseeable object of our faith must be figured if it is to appeal to our imagination and govern our feeling and conduct. We cannot adapt our conduct to a world that is wholly unknown; it must be known at least in symbol; in some fiction founded in fact and experience. So far as we have mistaken this fiction for fact, this symbol for the transcendent reality, we, too, have been disappointed, like the prophets of old.

The first Christians expected the Son of Man to appear in the clouds within a few days. After repeated disappointments, they remembered that God's days were a thousand years. In the year one thousand the old hope kindled again, but now we have practically abandoned all hope. Yet we have learnt something, namely, that any imaginable vision of the transcendent can be no more than symbolic. For this reason we are content with that in which Christ incorporated His religious "idea." We are less likely to take it literally than any new rendering of our own; more likely to understand it as a mystery of faith and not as historical foresight.

(c) RESURRECTION

The belief in spiritual immortality is, then, inseparable from spiritual religion; though, like such religion, it will clothe itself in the visible and imaginable forms of our present experience. If in some sense it is Christ who "brought life and incorruption to light," yet immortality, or resurrection (for they were not then distinguished) was already implied in the apocalyptic conception of the Kingdom of Heaven. It was the belief of the Pharisees, as opposed to the philosophical scepticism of the Sadducees. It had permeated the uncritical multitude. Jesus did not reveal it, but almost took it for granted. Men, who were not His disciples, were ready to believe that He Himself might be John the Baptist, or Elias, or Jeremiah, or one of the great prophets risen from the dead. It was not from Him that they had learnt this doctrine. According to the Gospel He Himself was not the first to rise. He and the prophets before Him had raised the dead, and at the moment of His own death, before He had risen, we are told that the graves were opened and that the bodies of the just arose. If S. Paul speaks of Him as the first-fruits of the dead he means first in dignity and causality, not first in time. Our modern apologists, with their idea of natural law and of miracle as a conquest of the power of nature by a Higher Power, by which conquest the existence of that Higher Power is proved, miss the meaning which Christ's resurrection had for those who had no idea of natural law or of any other power in nature than that of God. They speak as though the Apostles had doubted whether God could break through the determinism of nature and raise the dead, and as though their faith had been re-established by finding there was a power stronger than that of nature. This is to read later ideas into an earlier age.

In the first place, where there is no conception of nature as a rigid autonomous system of uniformities, there can be no conception of the preternatural. God was the sole mover of the physical world, which had no power of its own to oppose to His. He moved the sun or stayed it; He raised the storm or stilled it, as a man moves or stays what is within his strength and grasp. Order and uniformity were the self-imposed rule of His own action, and not the result of a necessity inherent in things. When God departed from His usual course He had no law or obstacle to overcome. The stilling of the sun was not more a divine action than its motion; no more an evidence of the existence of God. Departures from His usual habits were, of course, signs and wonders, but, in our modern sense, they were not miracles.

The Apostles had no doubt as to the resurrection of the body at the last day—a belief that they had not derived from Jesus. They did not regard it as a miracle in any sense, but, like every regular sequence in nature, a rule of Divine action, a part of God's freely chosen plan. In that plan death followed upon sin as regularly as, but not more necessarily than, night followed upon day. With the same regularity resurrection followed upon righteousness. It was only because righteousness came through the conquest of Satan, and the gift of the Spirit by the Son of Man, that S. Paul speaks of Christ as the cause and first-fruits of the Resurrection: "For since by man came death, by man came also resurrection of the dead," etc.

For the Apostles, the resurrection of Jesus meant that He who had claimed to be the destined Son of Man had been approved, justified and glorified by the Father, according to the rule by which resurrection is the established and almost natural consequence and proof of justice. What they had doubted was His claim to be the Christ; not the possibility of His resurrection. When He rose, their trust in Him, in their own redemption with and through Him, in His whole Gospel of the coming Kingdom and His own place in it, was confirmed and verified, not by an exceptional, but by a regular occurrence. Resurrection is the fruit of righteousness, and a tree is known by its fruit.

Thus S. Paul argues: "If there is no resurrection of the dead, neither hath Christ been raised." He assumes that only the just rise; he has to prove that Christ has been so justified by God. If the general law of resurrection be denied the premiss of his proof is gone. "If Christ hath not been raised then is our preaching vain, your faith also is vain"; there is no reason to believe that Jesus was what He claimed to be. By His resurrection He had been proved and made the Christ. Had He not risen, their faith in the coming Kingdom, the Son of Man and the resurrection of the just, would have remained intact; for it was not derived from Jesus. Only their faith in His Gospel of the nearness of the Kingdom and of His own identification with the promised Son of Man would have perished.

Yet it remains true that Christ brought eternal life and immortality to light, not as a new doctrine, but as a new fact. He brought it near, pressed it home, made it tangible and spiritually effectual, just as our unquestioning belief in our own mortality is made effectual by the death of those near to us, or by some proximate peril of death, and, from a mere assent of the mind, becomes an element in our character and conduct. For the Apostles the resurrection of Jesus was not merely that of one most near and dear; but of one through friendship with whom their own resurrection was secured. As such, it transfused their whole character with a hope that no temporal sorrow could trouble, and robbed death of all its terrors. It was this realisation of immortality that filled the early Church with a joy and enthusiasm that conquered the world and sent martyrs rejoicing to death and torment.

This, then, was the significance of the resurrection of Jesus for the Apostles. They had no doubt about God, or the possibility of superhuman wonders, or the coming of the Kingdom, or the resurrection of the dead, but only about the Messianic claim of Jesus; and this doubt was slain as soon as God approved Him in the established and universal way, i.e. by raising Him up.

And what are we to think of this alleged resurrection, which was undoubtedly the whole inspiration and strength of early Christianity, especially as it was considered a guarantee for the speedy end of all? The harvest had begun; the sickle was thrust in; the risen Christ was the first-fruits of the general resurrection.

THE APOCALYPTIC VISION OF CHRIST

Here we are on difficult ground. But it is a poor faith that dare not look difficulties straight in the face. If the Apostles were mistaken as to the immediacy of the End (and, of course, they were so in some sense) may they not have been mistaken as to the Christhood of Jesus, on which alone that expectancy was founded; and also as to His resurrection, on which their belief in His Christhood was founded? Might it not be put thus? If He has risen, He is the Christ; if He be the Christ, the end is near; but the end is not near, therefore He is not the Christ; therefore He has not risen. We have two interdependent facts—the resurrection of Jesus and the immediacy of the End. It is only by the sort of quibble that has made epochs out of six evenings and mornings of creation that we can pretend that the second of these facts has not been disproved by universal experience. Is the proof of the first anything like as strong as the disproof of the second?

The prophetic mind, as we have said, not only embodies its spiritual exigencies and desires in terms of present experience, in some glorified image of the visible world, but expresses the impatience and intensity of its desire in a foreshortening of time. It translates its felt spiritual nearness to the transcendental and eternal object of its faith into the image of things visible. So far as the prophet confounds the image with the transcendent that it symbolises, he is doomed to disappointment. The whole apocalyptic imagery of the Kingdom of Heaven; of the Son of Man; of the coming in the clouds; of the resurrection of the dead; of the Judgment in the valley of Jehoshaphat; of the immediacy of these events, is but imagery of the transcendent and unimaginable; of infinitely deeper realities. It is an attempt to figure our spiritual requirements in material form; to give them a language in which we can think of them and speak of them. For an embodied spirit they need embodiment if they are to be brought to bear on our present experience. It is the future moth trying to make itself intelligible to the present grub, in which it is dimly self-conscious and preparing for its coming life and environment.

The only manner in which the Christian Apocalypse can claim a greater finality and security than the repeatedly disappointed visions of the earlier prophets is in recognising the symbolic and inadequate character of all such visions. And this recognition advanced towards explicitness when the temporal interpretation of God's Kingdom gave place to the apocalyptic and quasi-transcendent. It advanced still further with Christ's insistence on the spiritual as the sole eternal reality. It only needed a gradual cleansing of the idea of spirit to complete the distinction between the imagery and the reality of the transcendent.

Now if we agree with Liberal Protestantism in taking symbolically what the early Church took literally, we differ in taking it all as symbolic of transcendental values and not of the moral order in this life. In so doing we only go more deeply into the original thought and get under its enveloping imagery; we do not go off on another line that is merely analogous. We hold to the transcendent Kingdom, and, while not discarding the imagery, we recognise that it is an envelope and not the substance. Hence we claim to be true to the "idea" of original Christianity. To this discrimination between substance and envelope we have been forced by the advance of human thought; by the progressive delimitation between the territories of subjective and objective, between vision and fact.

We need have no doubt that S. Stephen saw "the heavens opened and the Son of Man standing at the right hand of God." We have none as to the reality of such phenomena. We only ask: were they determined from without or from within; did they belong to that series of regular sequences which exists for all, or to that which exists for one alone? Did they reveal what we call the external world, or the spirit and faith of the beholder? were they true to an outward or to an inward reality?

When the mechanism of thought, on the one hand, and of physical nature on the other, was less understood, it was inevitable that the phenomena of the former series should be frequently intercalated in the latter. To attribute our own psychological nicety to the first century is an anachronism.

There can be no doubt as to the appearances of Jesus to His Apostles after death. Without them the faith, hope and enthusiasm of the early Church are inexplicable. It is plain that the Apostles intercalated the phenomena into those of the physical series, yet not without some sense of their otherness. He appeared and vanished like creatures of imagination; He passed through closed doors and rose in the air. S. Paul says: "Have I not seen Jesus our Lord?" yet describes that vision as existing for himself and not for those round him, as belonging to the subjective series of phenomena. His whole doctrine of the spiritual body shows the same consciousness. It is not the body that is sown and destroyed, it is not the body of flesh, it is a transcendental body, though figured in terms of the phenomenal world. He figures it as, in some way, growing out of the fleshly body, like corn from the perishing seed—as related to it in the same way that the transcendent order is related to the present order. And in all this he was answering the question: "How do the dead arise? with what bodies do they come?" He was answering those who mistakenly supposed that the resurrection phenomena had to be fitted in with the physical series. He tells them, in effect, that they do not belong to that series; that they proceed from an inward, not an outward, reality. Yet, however subjective may be the imaginative clothing of that reality, the reality itself is not necessarily subjective and private. The principles of truth and morality are inward, but not subjective; they are valid for all and not for one alone. God's Spirit works in every conscience, and, if our various pictures of its workings are subjective, they are pictures of something within us that is independent of us and is the same for all.

Shall we then be very far from S. Paul's thought if we say that the spiritual body is the imaginative embodiment of the spirit, the expression of the transcendent in terms of natural experience; just as the material or fleshly body is that which expresses itself in the phenomena of the physical sequence?

Among those images that exist for the subject alone we find the same difference as among those that exist for all and constitute the external world. There are some whose sequence and grouping answer to no observed regularity and evade our calculation and understanding. Thus it is with nearly all external phenomena for children and savages; and, to a great extent, for ourselves also. Thus, too, our dreams and a large part of our waking imaginations follow no intelligible order, and serve no end visible to our eyes.

And then there are other phenomena, of both series, that have meaning and purpose for us. Thus, between a mere dream and a vision, there is all the difference that exists between the casual and the purposeful. The subjective imaginings of the poet and painter are unified embodiments of active æsthetic needs. They are the work of the spirit, selecting its materials from the psychological stream of incoherent images, and ordering them in view of an end. The spirit is seeking its spiritual body, an expression of its transcendental end in terms of sensible experience. So, too, the images in which the religious idea incorporates itself are purposeful and not casual. They are twice removed from the subjectivity of dreams; first, as symbols relating to a reality; then, as relating to a reality which, though inward, is in no sense subjective, but even more objective than what we call the external world.

Yet if poetic or prophetic vision be purposeful, the purpose is not necessarily explicit and calculated. The strongest inspiration dispenses altogether with the assistance of reason and reflection, and embodies itself so spontaneously that the vision seems something given and imposed, and, as such, is all the more liable to be ascribed to the series of outward phenomena. A Dante often seems to describe what he saw, though, at other times, we feel that he is constructing something for us to see. And between pure spontaneity and pure elaboration there are all degrees of an elaboration of the spontaneous.

The resurrection of the just is an integral part of the apocalyptic scheme. We cannot treat the two apart; they enjoy just the same kind of truth and reality—either the same literalism or the same symbolic value, be it moral or transcendent. For the Liberal Protestant the resurrection is a symbol of the victorious survival of the morality of Jesus in the Church and the World. For the Liberal Catholic it is a symbol of the survival of the spiritual personality of Jesus in that transcendental world which pervades the visible order.

Those who accept it as a merely physical event in this lower plane of phenomenal reality must, in consistency, accept the rest of the apocalyptic vision in the same sense—must accept the advent in the clouds, the great assize in the valley of Jehoshaphat, as they were accepted by the Apostles and the early Church. What they actually saw could only confirm them in their literalism—they saw Jesus risen in physical form; they saw Him ascend to the physical heavens; they saw those heavens opened, like an awning, and Jesus standing at the right hand of the visible Father.

Now we may ask ourselves what spiritual significance and value could these phenomenal happenings possibly have for faith? Apart from some truly transcendental reality which they figure, and which alone is the object that explains and satisfies our spiritual unrest, what interest can physical phenomena and marvels have for religion? The physical resurrection and ascension could, at most, be signs and symbols of Christ's spiritual transformation, of the fulness of His eternal and transcendent life; they could never be its substance. Is it in physical radiance and power and subtlety and swiftness that our spiritual nature will find its explanation and satisfaction? Is it in the bric-à-brac, rococo Heaven of the Apocalypse of S. John that our souls are to find rest?

Even, then, though the Apostles regarded the resurrection phenomena as quasi-physical; even though they grasped the envelope and its content in the same hand; yet the substance was given to them by faith alone. What their bodily eyes beheld was but a symbol of a transcendent resurrection, visible only to the eye of faith. The inward experience, that thus expressed itself, was the recognition that the Divine Personality of Jesus—the Spirit that He was—cannot die; that it dwells in us all as something distinct from ourselves, ever claiming our absolute worship and obedience. In His mortality He had revealed the humanity and loving-kindness of that Spirit; He had clothed it in visible and fleshly form; He had given it a human voice. Henceforth, in the inward dictates of that Spirit, they recognised the "I say unto you" of the voice of Jesus of Nazareth; and the mysterious influence bore His human form and features. Plainly the symbol was accommodated to their apocalyptic ideas, to their belief in a quasi-physical Kingdom of Heaven, a quasi-physical resurrection of the just.

They had no doubt that the just would rise from their graves. There is no valid critical reason for denying that Jesus had predicted His resurrection as the pendent to His self-sought atoning death. All the trust and faith with which He had inspired them bade them expect that resurrection, which was to justify Him and His claim to be the

Son of Man. Their faith in His resurrection was kindled from His own. Moreover, it was fortified by the Scriptures. Even had He not appeared to them at all they ought to have, and might have, believed. This is the meaning of " Blessed are they that have not seen and yet have believed," and " O foolish men and slow of heart to believe in all that the prophets have spoken." The appearances seem to be viewed rather as a reward of faith than as a proof of the resurrection; to be a consequence, not an antecedent, of faith, in accordance with Christ's whole attitude towards miracles. While they doubted they did not see Him; their eyes were held. As soon as they believed they saw Him.

Have we not, then, every reason to believe that what they saw was a vision, the spontaneous self-embodiment, in familiar apocalyptic imagery, of their faith in His spiritual triumph and resurrection, in the transcendental and eternal order—a vision that was externalised by the very intensity of their faith, that seemed something given from outside; a vision that was purposive and symbolical of a reality which, though inwardly apprehended, was in no sense subjective; a vision that was divine, just because the faith that produced it was divine?

Of course criticism will not accept all the details

of these appearances; but it cannot deny their possibility and likelihood in relation to the mentality of the time and place; and it must admit enough to account for the birth of Christianity. Moreover, we may not look for consistency of detail between subjective expressions of transcendent facts, as between accounts of the same physical fact. Visions, besides, change even in the first telling; still more in the second and third. But they can remain true to the inward fact they symbolise.

Thus, as visions, the resurrection phenomena take their proper place in the Apocalypse of the Kingdom of Heaven. The alternative is to give physical value to the whole Apocalypse. The Resurrection thus becomes a visionary presentment of the truth of spiritual immortality; of the eternity and plenary expansion of that super-individual life that lies hid in the depths of our being; that strives vainly to express itself in terms of our psychic and organic life; that is the root of our discontent, not only with all that the world gives, but with all that it could ever conceivably give.

In the measure that a man is himself spiritual, his faith in eternal life is more irresistible. The faith of the Apostles in the resurrection of Jesus was the product of their own spirituality and of their estimate of the spirituality of Him who had opened their spiritual eyes and ears; of Him whom it was impossible that death should hold: "Thou wilt not give Thy Holy One to see corruption."

Christianity is then, pre-eminently, the Gospel of immortality and eternal life; not of a shadowy survival in Hades; not of a prolongation of a kind of existence that could never conceivably satisfy our deepest spiritual need; but of that spirit-life itself in its full self-consciousness. It brought home to men, as a felt and effectual reality, the notion of another life, which robbed this of all value except as related to it and illuminated by its nearness. It tempered and neutralised the proximate pessimism of the despairing spirit with an alternate optimism. It sweetened life's bitter waters with the wood of the Cross. It was a Gospel for the afflicted in soul and body, to whom it promised no temporal alleviation, no social paradise after an unending process of development, but eternal rest for their souls in the bosom of God. To thrust immortality into the background, as a dim possibility that has not much to do with our Christianity; to make the reign of morality on earth, in ourselves and in society, the whole meaning of the Kingdom of God and of eternal life, is to abandon, not religion, but the religion of Christ; it is to substitute a religious morality for a moral religion; to make what is conditional, principal; what is principal, subsidiary; it is to insist on what unites us to God rather than on union with God, whereof morality is but one of many conditions. The emphasis of Christianity is on the whole life of the Spirit, viewed as a divine and eternal life, to be fully revealed only in its proper transcendental environment.

If this truth did not originate with Christ, yet it was He who quickened it to active life and brought it home to humanity. Of this quickening His own realisation and vision of eternal life was the principal cause. To this was then added that realisation of it which, through the power of His personality, He communicated to His Apostles, issuing in their conviction as to His resurrection, and in the visions that were at once the effect and the confirmation of that conviction. Then, too, the tidings of the nearness of the Kingdom could not fail to bring a vivid realisation of the truth to a generation that had lost all faith in the present life; that had no belief in the panacea of progress; that viewed the world as given over to the Devil's dominion, to some iron law of failure and disappointment; that looked for remedy only in an "act of God" that should sweep away the old order at a stroke and bring in the new. This pessimism was the richest soil in which the hope of immortality could take root; and it was the concurrence of such despair of this life with such faith in the next that gave Christianity its initial impetus.

If, however, the attitude of the minority, who live deeply and fully, towards the present order is one of despair, the general mind is subject to periodic waves of elation and depression. At present the world that is heard and seen in public, elated with the success of science and the triumphs of invention, confident that what has done so much will do everything, is blind to the appalling residue of human misery and to the insoluble problems that are coming up slowly like storm-clouds on the horizon. Once more we are told that life will work out the cure of its own evils and change the world into Paradise; that progress will now run its course uninterruptedly, and will not, as ever in the past, be thrown back in spray, like a wave from an opposing cliff. Such a period is not one in which the Gospel of a transcendent life will meet with enthusiastic faith. Religion itself is apt to come to terms with the temper of the day. Immortality is thrust into the background. Christian civilisation takes the place of the Kingdom of God; and morality, that of eternal life. The Churches chatter progress, and the secular and clerical arm are linked together in the interests of a sanctified worldliness.

(d) THE IMMEDIACY OF THE KINGDOM

For the Apostles the resurrection of Jesus was a new pledge of the immediacy of the End—of the day when He who had risen and ascended should come in the clouds to proclaim His resurrection and Christhood to the whole world, and bring human history to an end. And it was this sense of immediacy, more than anything else, that changed the belief in eternal life from mere assent to an effectual motive, productive of a new sentiment and a new manner of living.

That the world passes away for each and for all —not only for man but for all humanity—is the motive for that Christian detachment which sets its affections on things above and not on things of earth. As a truth of reason and experience we do not doubt it. But only in rare moments, when we realise it, does it exercise its due influence on our affections and conduct, and show us life's true values and its illusions in a flash of light. Many a change in our character dates from such moments and is sustained by their repetition. Apart from them, we are tangled in dreams and throw our whole interest into them; and, if there be no transcendent life, we do well, for we are then but dreams ourselves. If we look to a waking; if we take our dreams with a question and a reserve, we shall spoil the little that we have. Let us rather try to believe that our race is eternal, and that its final beatitude on earth is the justification of all our moral endeavour—that conscience is no more than the specific instinct which compels us to work for the survival of the species *Homo sapiens*.

It was, then, the conviction that the Kingdom was at hand, even at the very door, that the harvest was ripe, the first-fruits already gathered in, that brought the multitude of believers face to face with the illusions of time and the realities of eternity, and transformed their whole outlook and sentiment.

And was it all no more than a providential mistake, to which Christianity owes the impulse that still carries it along?

Yes, so far as this temporal nearness of the visible "parousia" was confounded with the spiritual reality of which it was the symbol; so far as the apocalyptic vision was referred to the series of outward phenomena. But such visions are the creations of an inward reality that faith seizes through them. "All truth," says Isaac Pennington, "is a shadow except the last—except the utmost; yet every truth is true in its kind. It is substance in its own place, though it be but a shadow in another place—for it is but a shadow from an intenser substance—and the shadow is a true shadow, as the substance is a true substance." This we might well say of the successive efforts of religion to picture the transcendent. Each presentment is more substantial than its predecessor, but the last alone is substance, and this, man can never picture while he lives and thinks among shadows.

It is by dimness that the painter gives the impression of distance; what is clear seems near. The clearness of the prophet's insight, the keenness of his desire, make him feel that his ideals and visions are on the point of realisation. What he thus translates from spiritual into external values is his own nearness to the transcendent in the state of exaltation and inward tension. He feels Heaven pressing upon him. He gathers up time into the present Now of eternity. Hence the eye of his reason is magnetised by his interest. He can only see the signs of the end; earthquakes, wars, pestilences, social confusion and chaos—and when are they not to be seen in a world like this? while he is blind to everything else—to the forces of life that are ever in conflict with those of death. But the truth that he struggles with is the brevity, the comparative nothingness of human duration; the need to live as though death were knocking at the door. A clear intuition of the magnitude of the eternal and transcendent translates itself *imaginatively* into an unending tract of centuries, contrasted with one dying day; and *practically* into a certain detachment of the soul from things transitory.

Now this practical expression is subject to illusions, like to, and in part dependent on, those of the imaginative expression; and these illusions are answerable for a not unfounded prejudice against transcendental, other-worldly religion of every kind.

The conviction of the nearness of death will affect men differently. The purely unspiritual man may either be reduced to a state of sullen apathy, or, as has been observed in times of pestilence, driven to snatch the last crumbs of pleasure and excitement that life has to offer. The man of principle, whose religion is simply implicit and who looks to no life hereafter, will fulfil his duties perhaps more punctiliously than ever, with the exception of that of providing for his future years. Should the conviction prove mistaken his temporal career may suffer to some extent, but, on the other hand, the experience may have been a source of moral insight and strength well worth the temporal loss. If, however, he believes in and realises the life to come, there is always some danger lest his contempt of the world lead him to think too lightly of its duties. And this danger besets him in a lesser degree at all times. Whence a certain *de facto* contrast between the moral and the religious temperament. Neither scepticism nor faith takes the world seriously enough.

Now it cannot be taken too seriously if the seriousness be grounded on truth. But it is possible that a good deal of moral seriousness rests on illusion, just as does the immoral seriousness of the frivolous. It rests on the tacit assumption that this life is everything and an end in itself—a coherent self-explanatory whole; that it is working by a process of necessary development towards a perfect harmony; that the human race is eternal, and absolutely significant apart from the transcendent. This is, no doubt, a useful and fertile illusion and has produced genuine moral fruit in abundance. The moral, like the religious, sense must have some *Weltanschauung*, some imaginative scheme of things, if its energies are to have definite direction. And, plainly, we should live to some extent as though this illusion were truth. In the conflict between life and death, progress and decay, our energies should be wholly on the side of life. Not, however, because we believe that life in this order can ever be finally victorious over almighty death and oblivion, or that our noblest efforts are not doomed to eventual defeat, and to utter sterility for remoter epochs; but only because every moral effort has a transcendent and absolute value apart from its success or failure, and one that the certainty of eventual failure enhances rather than diminishes. A moral act faces inwards and outwards; it belongs to the transcendent world and to the visible; it has a soul and a body; an imperishable and a perishable value. So far as it is the latter that moves and stimulates us to exertion, it is an illusory motive. Its effect is to attach us to the transitory; to immerse us wholly in progress; to make earth our heaven, and humanity our God. The inward spring of all this heroism and effort is, no doubt, spiritual and transcendent; but it is not thus interpreted and felt. The eye is fixed on a dream of progress brought to perfection at the end of some final century. Hence a curious leadenness and solemnity, that often spoils moralism of this description; especially when it goes hand in hand with a deterministic view of the world, a rigid exclusion of every sort of contingency.

Against this sort of seriousness the sceptic rises in revolt. He cannot contemplate the withering immensities of stellar time and space; he cannot read the ominous testimony of the rocks; he cannot study the records of dead religions and civilisations; he cannot ponder the chaotic conditions of the present, and yet take the dream of triumphant progress seriously, or see more than the struggles of a drowning crew, trying to keep afloat as long as possible, before yielding themselves to the deep of oblivion. At most, morality may be the best way to keep afloat. If the sceptical view be hopeless, in default of faith, at least it preserves a sense of proportion, and holds an element of truth. If it favour a far lower worldliness than that of the moralist, it is relieved by a certain contempt of the world it embraces. It can better afford to look at life with both eyes and pronounce it very bad and not likely to be better. It has not to imagine a harmony where there is nothing but discord; or to look for a single aim, uniting a chaos of conflicting and independent ends.

And this modern and Western scepticism is only a return to the grey wisdom of the world-weary East. Five centuries before Christ it had learnt that the world's miseries were incurable, that its blessings were illusions, that its process was no progress, that the best cure was to die to it without fear of any resurrection. Immortality—the endless prolongation of this experience—is the

Buddhist's hell. Of any better experience he has no explicit hope, though it is impossible not to interpret his Nirvana as an attempt to express the transcendental life by way of negation—and, so far, rightly. Unlike ours, his morality and asceticism are inspired by the conviction that life is evil and not good. He seeks not to live more fully, but to die more fully; not to keep afloat, but to sink once and for all to the very bottom. His terror is lest, through his senses, he should become attached to the torture-wheel of life. He dare not die with a single attachment that would draw him back to earth again and be a seed of resurrection in his soul. Small wonder that the passive Buddha sits gazing with quiet amazement at our ant-like turmoil and activity, our hopes, our dreams, our moral struggles with the impossible, our terrible seriousness about shadows: " Are ye still without understanding ? "

If Buddhism be not explicitly a religion—for its very gods and heavens belong to the world of illusions and are still under the curse of existence—its scorn of the world implies something in man that the world can never satisfy; a hunger that can find no food; an ideal of truth and reality that revolts against illusion. Reason has brought it to the edge of a chasm that faith fears to leap. Hence its pessimism is final and not merely provisional. It can find no justification for the effort of progress; nothing but condemnation.

It is the Christian faith in spiritual immortality that changes this ultimately into a provisional pessimism, and balances an absolute detachment from the interests of the world by a provisional attachment to them. A provisional pessimism is the foundation of the Christian type of religious character. It is the soil in which the seed of the Gospel takes root and flourishes. Despair of this life is the counterfoil of our hope in another. It was no Buddhist, but the profoundly Christian Michael Angelo, who wrote—

> Fain would I sleep; fainer be dead as stone,
> While Wrong and Shame on every side abound;
> Stark, sightless, senseless! God, what a boon!
> Then wake, oh wake me not. Hush! Not a sound!

And the same note is struck by every great Catholic saint or hero whose pessimism, like that of the stern sculptor, reveals itself, not so much in contemptuous aversion from the world, as in a vigorous losing fight against the overwhelming forces of evil. In deference to the optimistic Gospel of progress, Christians are disposed in these days to modulate or silence this strident note of pessimism; to feel it as something excessive and mistaken, excusable in disorderly and catastrophic periods. But it is vain to deny that this note is as true to the Gospel of Christ as a cheerful belief in the world is discordant from it. For Christ the world was as good as finished and its final state was one of universal failure and illusion, not one of a proximate perfection that was all but Paradise. Well for the poor, the afflicted, the oppressed, who had lost all hope in it! Woe to the easy, the prosperous, the optimistic, who believed in it because they had themselves found it a soft place! From these the truth about it had been hidden; to those it had been revealed. The sharp discipline of bitter experience had taught the ignorant multitudes what the deepest philosophy learns only after much thought and labour. Hence it was the poor who were ready for the Gospel of another life—not for the Gospel of social development.

It is equally clear that the joy and hope of the early community rested on a basis of pessimism as to this world and its prospects. It was just tottering to its ruin, and, in the hope of a near eternity, its light and momentary tribulations were borne cheerfully and gladly; its gravest events and concerns were not taken seriously, nor as laden with all that importance attached to them by the moralist, whose faith is in life, whose hope is in development. In this sort of lightness of touch, which may easily be excessive, the Christian had something of the sceptic's unseriousness. It enters as an ingredient into that sort of charity which seems too easy-going in the eyes of the pharisaical rigorist — bearing, believing, hoping, enduring, all things; into that improvidence about temporal concerns, that indifference to injuries, that contempt of good or ill report, that Jesus commended both by word and example. What else could result from a conviction of the badness of the present life, combined with a vivid faith in the nearness of a better? Men will take a ghost seriously only till they find it is but a shadow.

Yet this emphasis on the other world, however necessary as a corrective, needed to be checked and balanced by a just estimate of the meaning and value of time in relation to eternity. He who said "Blessed are the poor, the hungry, the suffering," spent His life in relieving their needs; He who said "The night cometh," gave it as a motive for working while it was yet day; He who said "The Kingdom is at hand," was urging men to repentance and righteousness. At the Judgment the reward is not for those who have successfully turned earth into paradise and accomplished the impossible, but for those who have striven to alleviate its miseries; who have fought a despairing battle against the overwhelming forces of evil. It is not so much the actively evil, as the slack and apathetic, that are excluded from the Kingdom. Life, therefore, gains a new importance as the arena of the great "temptation"—of the conflict between the forces of Darkness and Light, Death and Life, Earth and Heaven; a conflict where Satan must first be victorious in the present order before God shall arise to scatter His enemies and establish His Kingdom. It is not so much by their efforts, as by their consequent failures and sufferings, that the saints are to hasten God's final intervention. In a way they are indifferent to success or failure, so long as they have striven with all their might. In that striving their spiritual personality is created and deepened; their union with God strengthened; their place in the transcendent order determined.

Far, then, from relaxing moral effort for the alleviation of earth's misery, the Christian faith, rightly apprehended, intensifies and purifies it. Those who fight only for victory grow slack when victory is hopeless. Those who fight for hate or for love will fight till they drop. Such has been the desperate energy with which typical Christian saints have combated life's evils, moral and physical—the energy of those who are masters and not slaves of their purpose; whose provisional attachment to life's interests is subordinate to an ultimate detachment; who use the world as not using it; who strain for success and smile when they fail. Like Christ they serve; like Him they are lords and masters of what they serve. They are not immersed in the clay which they are moulding but stand well outside it and above it.

But this faith has not always been rightly apprehended. In the early Church, if the temporal nearness of the End was a stimulus to the wise, it was, to the foolish, a plea for apathy and idleness—to those, namely, who looked on success and victory as the sole justification of labour and conflict, and who would waste no care on a vanishing world. Even the wise, so far as they grasped the symbol and the truth in the same act of faith, and confounded the temporal with the transcendental and absolute nearness of the Kingdom, justifiably neglected provision for a future that would never come. They did not occupy themselves in far-reaching social and ecclesiastical schemes, with a view to cutting the roots of evils to come in later centuries. Sufficient for the day was the evil thereof. The chance of a morrow was slight. And even when the thought of temporal immediacy had lost its influence, through delays and disappointments, the realisation of an eternity, near for the individual, was too often misapplied to the prejudice of energy, and the approach of night taken as a reason for wasting the last hours of the day.

But this sort of abuse and misapprehension is heartily condemned, not only by Christ Himself, but by the saints of all ages, who have been characterised by a burning activity and zeal in well-doing. To the pure moralist, engrossed in conduct and progress, a good deal of their activity may seem misplaced. But in spite of many orientalisms and ascetical fallacies in its application, the principle of Christian action makes for the fullest expansion of man's transcendental and spiritual nature in every direction. It recognises the Divine, not only in conduct and in relation to man's moral progress, but also in thought and in feeling; it lives for the æsthetic and intellectual as well as for the ethical "ought" and ideal. It is the foe of falsehood and ugliness as well as of wickedness; it sees in all of them the principle of evil, death and decay. It turns in despair from this world to the transcendent in search of the synthesis, not only of duty and happiness, but of truth and loveliness, and of goodness with both. It is through religion that it unites these interests and finds courage to struggle for their harmony, though it can only succeed in diminishing their discord.

The truth, then, that Christianity symbolises, under the temporal nearness of the End, is a fundamental principle of the best spiritual life—the principle of an attachment to the world's highest interest, at once strengthened and subdued by an attachment to an eternal and transcendent life, symbolised by the Kingdom of Heaven. The abuse of this truth, to the prejudice not only of the rights of this life but of the proper development of spiritual personality, is answerable for a complete inversion of view as to the relation of religion to the world. So far as religious ethic identifies our duties in life with the Will of God, it asserts a neglected principle of Christianity. But so far as it identifies the moral with the religious life and the Kingdom of Heaven with the ideal term of an endless social and moral process, it is a flat contradiction of the Gospel of Christ. Far from freeing us, it ties us hand and foot with the iron bands of duty, to that which sooner or later must follow the law of mortality. Humanity is as mortal as any son of Adam. Be it a hell or a Paradise, the world shall pass away like a dream or a cloud, or the track of a ship in the waters.

(e) THE SON OF MAN

The Kingdom of Heaven; His own Christhood; the temporal immediacy of the End, were the three organic constituents of the Apocalypse of Jesus. Of these the last was in some sense principal in point of motive power and inspiration, though His Messianic secret was undoubtedly the central and solely original factor. The first belonged to the apocalyptic tradition; the last, to the preaching of the Baptist.

Now this view of the immediacy of the Kingdom cannot be accepted as of literal and phenomenal value, but as a vision symbolic of a transcendental reality that does not admit of literal expression; and we must accord the same kind of truth and reality to the organic whole as to each of its parts. We know, experimentally, that, in the year 30, the End was not nearer in time than was the first advent in the year 1879 B.C. If "near" stood for 1879 years, it was not used in its literal sense. And though it does not admit of the same sort of experimental evidence, we are equally clear that the apocalyptic delineation of the Kingdom of Heaven is but a symbol and vision of the transcendent. We cannot possibly stop short and suppose that the image of the Son of Man belongs to the order of literal and phenomenal values, any more than does the Great Dragon or the other mysterious beings that figure in the same vision.

It is well to reflect that the same must be said of "the Heavenly Father" and of all our ideas and images of God which do not, like our ideas of things within experience, correspond to something within that order of experience. They are to all intents and purposes "visions" of that transcendent reality which alone answers to our spiritual needs and instincts. If truth be the correct anticipation of a possible experience, it is our spiritual needs that are true to God, not the ideas and images in which we try to explain those needs in terms of present experience, and by a heaping together of incompatibles. Yet if the anticipation of phenomenal experiences, implied by a literal acceptance of these images, be incorrect; if, so taken, they are illusory; they have none the less a certain practical truth, in that they enable us to anticipate and control spiritual experiences and to adjust our conduct to the transcendent world. They are not arbitrary but natural symbols; as effects are symbols of their causes and parts of their wholes. However assisted or impeded by art and reflection, it is the transcendent that shapes its own symbol and image in the human mind. Spontaneously every spiritual need and movement pictures its own object and cause in the terms of imagination. Were they arbitrary signs like x and y, one would be as good as another. But the Father of Jesus is a far richer and truer symbol of God than the War-God of early Israel. It is the result of progressive self-revelation on the part of the transcendent. As the spirit grows in man his symbolism grows truer and more spiritual. "Truer," because it gives a fuller anticipation and control of spiritual experience. But truer also because, though unlike in kind, it is, in another kind, more analogous to God—as a symphony might resemble a picture either more or less.

So with the hypotheses of physical science, which are fictions founded in fact. Not one of them is absolutely true as resting on a complete comprehension of the whole universe. But one is truer than another as yielding a wider anticipation and control of experience; and that it does so means that it is, in some greater degree, *like* nature—not merely analogous, since the fiction and fact are in the same order. Aided by art and reflection, they are suggested, criticised and improved by experience. They are self-revelations of physical nature; to which science is related as is theology to Divine revelation.

It is not merely that in acting *as if* God were our father we shall gain certain beneficial results, but that God has revealed Himself to us under this figure, whose analogous truth is the explanation of those results. Nature is not actually a machine nor an organism, but, were she not so inclusively or equivalently, those fictions could not yield such fruitful results. They must at least be founded in fact. And so with all our symbols of the Divine, as far as they are spiritually fruitful.

Moreover, as regards the transcendental, we are not as blind men trying to build up the colour-world in terms of music. We have a dim sense of light and darkness whose purpose we do not rightly understand, whose potentialities we cannot imagine. In our spiritual life we have the rudiments of a transcendent experience. We know at least the sort of stuff that Heaven is built out of, as music is built out of sound. We can say: As a symphony is to a sound, so is the unknown world of colour to this dim sensation of light. We can say: As nature is to a clod, so is the spiritual world to our own spirit. We have three terms for our analogy. Else religion would have no *raison d'être*. We do not need, we cannot desire, to adjust ourselves to the absolutely diverse—to what cannot affect us in any way. If there be not a Divine element in us, the Divine does not concern us.

For those that reflect, it is no doubt advisable that they should recognise the symbolic character of their conceptions and images of the Divine, lest, finding them discordant with the natural understanding, they should reject them as void of all value. But the vast majority take the symbol and reality indistinctly as one thing, without any prejudice to their spiritual life. Even fairly educated believers accept, not only their symbol of God, but nearly all the apocalyptic imagery of the Christian faith, as so much literal fact. It is so indistinguishably associated with their religious life and experience, that they cling to it with the same faith, and put it on the same plane of reality. For them it is revealed phenomenal fact. Only here and there, where the imagery has come into patent conflict with knowledge, is it discarded—along with the transcendent truth it symbolises. People who no longer believe in devils go on believing in angels; they deny Hell but they accept Heaven. The literal acceptance of the former offends their rational or ethical sense. They are sure about God; but not so sure about the Trinity. This transitional state between consistent literalism and consistent symbolism is distressing and dangerous. What retards the process of liberation is just the fear of losing the experience and guidance so long associated with simple literalism. But only when the liberation is completed will it be possible to go back with safety and profit to the integrity of the Christian revelation, and realise its truth as a guide to spiritual experience and a vehicle of transcendental meanings.

Refine and purify our conception how we will, we think of even our own spiritual self under the analogy of an individual bodily thing, a plexus of sensible phenomena. Strive how we will, we think of God in terms of our own spirit so conceived. And we think of the relation between them under the analogy of some relation that obtains in the world of space alone. Identity or diversity are but figures and visions as applied to the transcendent. Their truth or falsehood is practical. We must act and feel, in some respects, as if there were an identity; in others, as if there were a diversity. Till we see what corresponds to our symbols, we have no idea of what answers to the relation of those symbols to one another.

And so when we come to the relation between Jesus and the Son of Man; between the Son of Man and God. Of these three terms, two are symbols of the transcendent.

The necessity of finding in Jesus a German Liberal Protestant, guided entirely by the light of a sweet, nineteenth-century reasonableness, requires us to ignore everything in the Gospel that suggests the visionary or the ecstatic, even though to do so make the narrative incoherent and unintelligible. When He called Himself the Son of Man, we are told it was because He felt Himself so entirely human—the Man *par excellence*. When He called

Himself the Son of God, it was because all men were sons of the common Father; and the Man *par excellence* was, therefore, the Son of God *par excellence*. A more drastic and objective criticism has shattered the beautiful simplicity of this tidy little system, obtained by a liberal use of the pruning-hook.

We do not need the Johannine and Pauline writings, we need only to read the Synoptics in the light of contemporary apocalyptic conceptions, to learn that Jesus considered Himself as of a superhuman nature, and as differing in kind from other men. It was a secret He eventually shared with His Apostles; it was the secret of His ascendency over them; it was a faith with which He inspired them. If the least in the Kingdom was above the greatest born of women, above the chief of prophets and saints and martyrs, He Who knew Himself to be the greatest in the Kingdom could hardly regard Himself as a mere prophet—a man among men.

The "Son of Man" was a heavenly being, mediatorial between God and man. He was the Power of God, by which Satan's power was to be broken and the Kingdom of Heaven to be established on earth. To Him all judgment was committed by nature. Like the Spirit of God, He was conceived vaguely, and, without prejudice to the Divine unity, as an emanation from God; the Arm of the Lord. What trouble later theology had with these emanations is testified by the Athanasian Creed—which attempts to satisfy reason while preserving the apocalyptic vision in its integrity, and which presents no difficulty when we remember that our rational concepts of the Divine are not less symbolic than our imaginative visions.

Jesus believed that He was destined to be revealed to all the world in the clouds of heaven, as the Son of Man. Probably, if not certainly, He understood this destination as more than moral or decretorial, as an inherent potentiality of His spirit. Already He spoke and acted as God's plenipotentiary. He forgave sins, because He knew Himself to be the "Son of Man" to whom all judgment had been committed; He judged the sacred Law; He called men to Himself; He bade them imitate Him; all this points to a sense of present, and not merely of prospective, superhuman dignity. Not till He was glorified, however, would He be technically the Christ and assume the full functions of the Son of Man.

Now it is idle to contend that this was something secondary in the self-consciousness of Jesus; a little touch of the megalomania so frequently attendant on genius and on the realisation of unusual influence and power; a fiery tongue of fanaticism, shooting up from the pure flame of faith. He does not begin as an ethical teacher or a prophet, and then warm up to new and astounding pretensions. His attitude is the same throughout, and is just such as consists with the secret consciousness of His Messianic dignity. That consciousness is the cause, and not the effect, of His soul-compelling power. His belief in Himself makes others believe in Him. The saint, the prophet, is ever self-obliterating. His strength is God's, not his own. He draws men to God, not to himself. He says "Thus saith the Lord," and not "But I say unto you." He claims to be only the servant of all, not also their Lord and Master. If Jesus believed Himself but man, He was no saint. But He felt He was more. And even those who did not share His Messianic secret felt and yielded to the authority with which He spoke. They asked themselves: "What manner of man is this?" What won their love and affection was the lowliness and gentleness of one whom they felt, through an irrepressible emanation of His own self-consciousness, to be mysteriously great and strong and holy.

We must recognise, then, that Jesus was conscious of Himself as in some way mediatorial between the transcendent world and the souls of men; that He felt, not merely His own union with God, but the power of uniting other souls to Himself, and, through Himself, with God; that this mission was imposed on Him from above; that He was set as a magnet for souls, which, magnetised through Him, should draw and magnetise others, till the whole of redeemable humanity, in Him, with Him, through Him, should be drawn back to God. This was the nature of His spiritual exigency, the bread for which He hungered—to accomplish the great atonement; to overthrow sin and Satan; to establish the Kingdom of Heaven; to banish the night of time; to bring in the day of eternity. No doubt this desire to redeem, this power to draw and to magnetise, belong to the spiritual nature as such, and to every man in the measure that his spiritual life has become explicit. Its source is the Divine nature itself. But no ordinary man, however possessed by the Divine Spirit, could feel himself to be the sole redeemer, mediator and source of redemption and mediation, in no need himself of redemption and atonement. Of this inward experience of Jesus, in which He felt Himself identified immediately with the Divine Source of Redemption, we can say nothing. We may rest satisfied that, when He claimed to be one with the Father, it was in no merely moral sense of accordant wills; but had reference to some mystical experience, some intuition of sameness in otherness.

Every such spiritual experience tends to translate itself into symbolic ideas and images, and, where strong and intense, to invest these images with the objectivity ascribed to dreams and visions. And the nature of the vision, as is proved by a thousand examples, depends on the religious ideas and images already to hand. These make the religious language of the seer; the words in which he must embody his experience for himself and for others. The current religious language in which Jesus thought and spoke was that of the prophets and apocalypses. The Kingdom of Heaven; the Son of Man, the Messiah; the Kingdom of Satan; the final catastrophe—these were the categories, under which His spiritual experience had to be ranged. Hence His sense of universal and supreme mediatorship between God and Man, of identification by love and sympathy with each of the terms to be united, could find no apter symbol than that of the prophetic Son of David, united to and "possessed" by the Heavenly Son of Man, or Son of God.

To transfer to the transcendental order the relations that obtain between the imaginative symbols of spiritual experience, is the same sort of fallacy that projects our scientific hypotheses into the physical world; or gives a real existence to our abstractions and general ideas. All we can say of such fictions is that they are founded in fact and reality. But where that reality is transcendent and spiritual, our fictions have only the truth of analogy—of parallels in another order of reality. Hence all our theology of the Incarnation deals, not with transcendent realities, but with the visions or revelations in which they are symbolised. Its purpose is to preserve the original force and usefulness of that symbolism; to secure its correct rendering for other ages and peoples; to make it coherent with itself and with the equally symbolic ideas of rational theology. We simply do not know what our own spirit is, or what the transcendent world is to which it aspires, or its relation to that world and to other spirits. What we do know is the impress they leave on a mind adapted to the world of physical phenomena.

The value of all these symbols and hypotheses is in the extent to which they anticipate and control that order of experiences on which they are founded; and every new success deepens that foundation and strengthens our faith. The faith in His own Christhood that Jesus, by the power of His personality, was able to plant in His Apostles, has been continually reinforced by the experience of those who have found Him, in effect, their

Redeemer, the Lord and Master of their souls, their Hope, their Love, their Rest—in short, all that they mean by God. For them He has become the effectual symbol or sacrament of the transcendent, through which they can apprehend the inapprehensible—the Eternal Spirit in human form.

The Messiahship of Jesus is, then, the symbolic expression, in terms of apocalyptic imagery, of certain transcendent realities—of the spiritual experience of Jesus as to His own relation to God and to men; and of the experiences of Christians as to their own relations to God and to Jesus. It is a visionary presentment of a transcendental truth, which we can present to ourselves in no other way; which we see *per speculum et in ænigmate*, but not *facie ad faciem*.

Theology is right in trying to make our symbolism coherent with itself and to preserve it from corruption. But when it strives to make it coherent with rational knowledge and outward experience, it forgets its symbolic character, and tends to pervert either revelation or knowledge, or both, in the interests of an impossible synthesis. In the orthodox and metaphysical formula of the Godhead of Christ we find, at most, a negative intellectual value combined with a positive pragmatic value. According to the latter, we are to bear ourselves towards Christ as towards a person possessed at once of a perfect human and a perfect Divine nature. According to the former, we are not to think of Him as two persons in only moral agreement; nor as a human person with extraordinary supernatural endowments; nor as a Divine person under the illusory appearances of humanity; nor as the Divinity substituted for a human soul in a human body. In short, the formula excludes every previous attempt to find a positive conception of the relationship of human and Divine in Jesus and to justify, intellectually, the Christian sentiment and attitude in regard to Him. There is little doubt but that those previous formulas, with all their incoherency and inadequacy, were attempts to justify Christian experience and feeling. It is plain that the disciples felt the strange and superhuman in Jesus as well as the human; that they feared as well as loved; that they found Him irresistible in His authority and power over their souls; that they reverenced Him as an incarnation of conscience, as a source of conversion and spiritual strength; that He possessed and governed them as a lover is possessed by the beloved.

It was some experience of this sort that the early Church strove to understand and explain. But the finally accepted formula is rather a statement of the problem than a solution. It insists on factors that the earlier formulas had neglected, and shows their insufficiency. But its solution, by way of a distinction between Nature and an unknown something called Personality, to which we can give no more positive content than to an algebraic x, simply leaves the metaphysical problem open and forbids further useless discussion. It prescribes a way of speaking and a way of acting in accordance with traditional sentiment and practice.

It is, however, possible to get some more positive idea of the "Messianic self-consciousness of Jesus" from the psychological side. The metaphysical categories of *ousia* and *hypostasis* were far from the Jewish mind. The psychological category of "possession" was familiar, and has, in our own days, received a coherent interpretation. The prophet was, for the time being, " possessed " by the Holy Spirit; the demoniac by the Evil Spirit. For the moment his psychological personality was submerged, and its place taken by a foreign personality, that governed his speech and action, and used his organism for its own purposes. We have come to understand the experience thus interpreted and to bring it under law. Normally we are solicited, prior to every free action, by various inclinations, motives and passions, and, amongst them, by the moral or religious motive, that is, by the voice of conscience. At this stage they are, as it were, outside us—objects of possible volition. They inhibit one another's actuation by their incompatibility. To choose one of the proposed actions means to allow it to absorb the central and greater part of the field of consciousness; to push its competitors to or over the margin of consciousness; to throw away our liberty as regards this particular attraction or impulse and yield ourselves to its force. In short, we allow it to possess us and actuate itself through us. Yet, in so doing, we are free; we have not been captured but have yielded ourselves; we can undo what we have done and release ourselves from the force that, for the moment, is incarnate in us. It is but a moment in the history of our personality, colouring and coloured by all that has gone before and that is still confusedly present in the background.

But there are abnormal states, where we are carried away by the violence and vividness of some strong desire or passion, to the utter exclusion of every other consideration, and to the complete obliteration of our whole past. We forget who we are and where we are; we are reckless, if not mad, for the moment; we are literally possessed, and beside ourselves, with anger, or fear, or enthusiasm, and become incarnations of those passions. The psychological "I," that speaks and acts, is not the

"I" that was, but is personified anger or fear. Thus the fanatic is one who is carried by his fiery zeal to a contempt and oblivion of every rational and moral consideration. His state is morbid, because the religion that absorbs his personality is not a pure religion, and often because the absorption is not due so much to the strength of the object as to the mental weakness of the subject— to his inability to hold out against perfectly normal solicitations. There are, however, solicitations of such strength as to overcome the resistance of the strongest and best-balanced mind. If it be an evil solicitation, it is the sufferer's misfortune but not his fault. If it be a good one, it is a grace but not a merit. In either case the normal psychological personality is extruded and the "I," which speaks and acts, is that of a good or evil spirit incarnate —to use the Jewish category.

The perfection man aims at, but never attains, is to yield himself freely, at all times, to the solicitations of conscience and of the Spirit of God, so that his motives and interests shall be subject and serviceable to the Divine and universal interest. This subjection may become habitual, but it is always free and revokable. The solicitation may be strong to the point of enthusiasm, but it is not overwhelming and destructive of his psychological personality. He is one thing; his conscience another. He may confidently say, "Thus saith the Lord," but he will not say, "*I* say unto you." That could be the utterance only of one whose normal psychological personality had been extruded by the overwhelming strength of the Spirit; of one who was literally God-possessed or conscience-possessed; in whom the " I " that speaks is simply conscience incarnate. To say that such a person is not free is to forget that he does not even exist; that the only personality there, is a divine personality, in possession of a human nature, and realising its unattainable divine ideal. That personality is free with the freedom of God and within the limits of conscience. Outside those limits it cannot go.

This, perhaps, gives us some little clue to the Messianic self-consciousness of Jesus; to His strange spiritual power over the souls of men; to His claim to be a revelation of the "humanity and benignity of God," which men would not believe in till they saw and felt it; to His claim to forgive sins, to give eternal life, to call men to Himself as if to God, to be their Lord and Master as well as their servant. And, if this be so, is not the breach between the Synoptics and the Fourth Gospel more apparent than real? is not the latter merely the substitution of Hellenic for Jewish categories in order to explain the same unique—we cannot say inconceivable—experience? Could not the Spirit incarnate in Jesus say : " I and the Father are one," " He that hath seen Me hath seen the Father," " I am the Truth and the Life," " He that hath the Son hath the Life"? Could not an apostle have hailed Him " My Lord and my God"?

Thus when we freely yield ourselves to the solicitations of the Spirit, we yield ourselves to the Personality that was incarnate as Jesus, whose humanity and benignity are revealed to us through that Incarnation, and, making ourselves members of Jesus, we lend our humanity, soul and body, to the service of that Personality.

We know that He did not escape the charge of fanaticism on the part of His nearest and dearest; still less, no doubt, on that of the sceptical Sadducees or of the more or less fanatical Pharisees. It is renewed by many of our modern Gospel-critics. But it is a charge universally levelled against any man who is enthusiastic and intransigent in the cause of truth and justice. In such a charge, however, we have evidence that He showed symptoms of that monoideism which is good or evil according to the idea or spirit in question, and according as the will yields to an irresistible or a normally resistible solicitation. The strongest man may be possessed and driven by the Spirit of God, but between him and the fanatic there is nothing in common, for the rule of the Spirit is the perfection, not the destruction, of rational life.

(f) GOD AND SATAN

If the nearness of the Kingdom and the Messiahship of Jesus are the substance and centre of the Christian revelation, various other subsidiary apocalyptic ideas need interpretation. We are confronted by an acute dualism of God and Satan in the quasi-physical other-world that does duty for the transcendent order. The conflict of Good and Evil in the present order is but the reverberation of a battle, raging in the invisible world, between the hosts of the Lord and those of Satan. When Jesus saw Satan fall as lightning from Heaven, it was a sign that the power of Evil on earth was practically killed in its root. The remnant of Satan's army still lingered in hiding. But they knew that their hour was come and that the Kingdom of God was upon them. They fled in terror at the word of Jesus, knowing that He was the Christ, the Heavenly Son of God. In this view Satan was the cause of sin; sin, the cause of mortality; mortality, the cause of sickness, sorrow and suffering. Opposed to Satan and his ministers was

God's Holy Spirit and His angels. As sin was a "possession" by Satan, so righteousness was a "possession" by the Holy Ghost. Man was free to yield his members as servants either to Sin or to Righteousness. He could not be his own; he must yield to one "possession" or the other. Thus man and the world are regarded as a territory for whose possession the invisible powers are struggling. Jesus beheld all the kingdoms of the earth usurped by Satan; all men born his possession, as being the children of those who had yielded up their liberty to him. He saw a world that was tied hand and foot and incapable of delivering itself; He saw men the slaves of sin, longing in vain to be free. Such was the pessimism of the Apocalypse.

Yet the struggle was not over. There was an ever dwindling band of just men, possessed by the Divine Spirit, free servants of God, who, in blind faith and trust, flung themselves desperately against the victorious forces of Evil, confident that, sooner or later, God, moved by their sufferings in His cause, would arise to scatter His enemies and establish His Kingdom. Here was the optimism of the Apocalypse.

The conflict has, therefore, a visible and an invisible side—as it were, a body and a soul. At root it was one between the Spirit of Evil, manifest in sin, death and sorrow, and the Spirit of Holiness, manifest in righteousness, immortality and joy. At the final crisis God, moved by the sufferings of His Saints (and of His Messiah) would pour forth the fulness of His Spirit on all flesh, before whose power the Spirit of Evil, after a final and desperate struggle, would fall. The Son of Man would gather the children of the Spirit into the Kingdom and drive the children of Satan into Hell; and thus the kingdoms of this world would become the Kingdom of God and His Christ, and be delivered from the usurpation of Satan.

So far is this *Weltanschauung* removed from our modern way of taking things that, though it is written broad over the face of the New Testament, the present-day Christian does not see it there as a whole, and is simply perplexed by the several fragments as he comes across them. All this casting-out of devils he could dispense with, as with something irrelevant and intrusive. We no longer regard a man's sickness as the fruit of some sin, by which he has become possessed of the Devil. Nor, if it be a congenital ailment, do we ascribe it to the sin of his parents, or some foreseen sin of his own. We seek physical causes for physical effects. We have recourse to the doctor and not to the exorcist. We do not believe that man is naturally immortal, and mortal only through sin ; we do not believe that physical immortality and resurrection are the due and quasi-natural consequences of righteousness.

And yet is our arrangement of the Whole any the less a fiction because it is a better one, because it unifies a greater extent of experience? Have we got, or shall we ever get, to more than a symbolic explanation of the great world drama —the conflict of Good and Evil? As compared with the Babylonian myth of Marduk and Tiamat and earlier legends, the apocalyptic view is inspired by a far deeper moral and religious sense, and its true values are to be looked for in the depth of the human spirit and not in the understanding. Take it as sober phenomenal reality and it must prove, as it has so largely proved, an obstacle to intelligence and to a true comprehension and use of the natural order. Take it as an effort of the spiritual life to express itself in the imagery of a certain place and time, and it still serves its purpose of registering that spiritual attitude, of fixing a direction of will, a character of sentiment—an entire "psychosis."

That good men cling to its literal truth, as they still do to some extent, is due to the fact that it is so intimately bound up with such a psychosis ; with those deep spiritual experiences that they cannot imagine incorporated in any other form. To admit that their God, their Satan and their Heaven are symbols is, for them, to deny the reality of their spiritual life—the firmest reality they know.

Imagine it how we will, life is a struggle between good and evil influences. Within ourselves we find a disinterested, forceful love of truth, goodness and beauty and their synthesis, that is thwarted and opposed by other forces within and around us. In the measure that we are spiritual, we realise that this love is doomed to disappointment and starvation in the present order; that it is overwhelmed by anti-spiritual forces. We are ourselves dominated by a strong anti-spiritual, individualist, self-centred tendency, the foe of order and universal love. We see this selfish, narrow, grasping temper wrecking the happiness of mankind at large and making hell all round it. Something in our spirit—its very craving for truth and justice—tells us that the prevailing divorce between inward and outward happiness is a flaw and disorder in life; that the suffering of the innocent is an evil, and that the whole world is drowned in an ocean of such injustice. We cry out for the triumph of the spirit; for deliverance from this body of death; for the end of this conflict, the conquest of this dualism; for the

Kingdom of God. And in our very despair we fight more vehemently, confident that, somehow or other, spirit must win; and that our efforts unite us more closely with the transcendent, where we shall find what we have here sought in vain, and in the measure that we sought it. Little as we know of the transcendent, beyond our own dim spiritual experience and its imaginative symbols, we feel that the world and its history come from, and return to, that hidden realm, and get their ultimate significance thence; that, so far as the conflict between Good and Evil is moral, and not merely phenomenal, it refers to an absolute, eternal and, therefore, transcendent order.

If the ultimate good, that determines moral right and wrong, were merely the eventual blessedness of our race upon earth, we should have no reason to feel that life's drama had its transcendent side. But the absolute, imperative, superhuman, super-temporal interest, to which the dictate of conscience (ethical, intellectual or æsthetic) points, translates itself inevitably into the picture of a battle in Heaven for the souls of men.

Dependent on the sense of the transcendent and universal significance of our free acts, is the sense of sin. No doubt it has been perverted by unworthy, non-moral, or even immoral, conceptions of God as arbitrary, vindictive, ambitious and cruel. Against these perversions a remedy has been sought in a purely rational and wholly inadequate interpretation of the experience of guilt. The view of sin as merely a trespass against our own higher interest and that of society, and, still more, the view of it as a mistaken judgment, not as a free self-determination, have weakened the sense of sin and left a real element of our inward experience without expression or explanation.

In apocalyptic thought, sin was an act by which a man yielded himself to the possession of Satan; sided with all the forces of Evil against the forces of Good; became an enemy of God and exposed himself to the destruction that would at last overwhelm the hosts of darkness. The significance of the act lay far less in the injury that might result to the doer and to society—results difficult to calculate and realise, and often imperceptibly minute—than in its absolute value as a defiance of the spiritual and transcendent, an act of hostility to God and of solidarity with Satan.

I do not think it can be denied that this view recognises an experience which belongs to religion even in its cruder forms, and which grows stronger and purer as man rises morally and spiritually. If religion adjusts him to the transcendent, sin is the essence of irreligion, and the forgiveness of sin the central aim of religion. Sin belongs to religion, not to morality. It is a severance of wills—Divine and human—a breach of union. Morality is but the subject-matter of the quarrel. Similarly, Righteousness, in the sense of Justification, acceptance by God, is a religious transcendental value, of which morality is but a condition or occasion, and Divine grace or mercy the cause.

By a loss of the sense of sin man's whole spiritual tone is impoverished, the significance of his life and conduct loses all relation to eternity, it bears only on the relative and transitory, on that which ultimately does not matter. He no longer lives in the transcendent but is wholly immersed in himself and in humanity. It was a gain to recognise morality as the will of God and to bring the two interests together; to purify and moralise religion; to supernaturalise and sanctify morality. But to substitute morality for religion was to fall back to earth again, after having essayed the sky; it was to rob morality of all the reinforcement it derived from the religious motive, from faith, hope and love; to leave its idealisms an easy prey to utilitarian criticism; to destroy the only motive that will make men fight, not less but more eagerly, in the face of ultimately inevitable defeat. That motive is faith in the transcendent value and significance of our moral efforts, independently of their success or failure.

(g) THE IDEA OF ATONEMENT

That the sufferings and persecutions of the saints were "precious in the sight of the Lord," that they moved Him to arise in their defence and overthrow the Kingdom of Satan, is a dominant idea of the Apocalypse. Yet it seemed as though some mysterious law of justice demanded an overbalancing of the demerits of the wicked by the merits of the saints, before God could intervene. The hour of that intervention was hastened by works of repentance, by deeds of righteousness, by sufferings for justice' sake. It was retarded by new sins and offences. Thus the various postponements of the great Day were ascribed to sin and laxity. The repentance preached by the Baptist and by Jesus was not merely to prepare for, but to hasten, the Kingdom—to take it by storm.

But if the unmerited sufferings of all the just had a certain atoning value, those of Jesus were not merely those of the most just of men, but those of the Messiah—of the Heavenly Son of Man incarnate in the Son of David. He was to the just as a shepherd to his sheep. Like a good shepherd, He gave Himself to be torn by the wolf that they might escape: "If therefore ye seek Me, let these go their way." His death filled up the cup of Satan's iniquity and moved God to pour forth His Spirit for the final destruction of the works of darkness, preparatory to the End. It was a weight thrown into the balance that the sufferings of the saints could never have turned. It was only through the blood of Jesus that the cry of Abel's blood was heard.

Now were sin but a moral disorder, bringing no sense of guilt or estrangement from the Divine Will, the remedy would be largely in our own power. It would be a mistake to go on crying over our past moral failures. What is past is irreparable. The only sensible sort of repentance would be a new life. But, in the light of religious experience, sin is an estrangement of spirit from spirit, the breach of a mutual bond. It is not enough to stretch forth our hand, we need an assurance that it will be grasped. We may long to be on God's side again, but till we are accepted we feel cut off from the organism of the spiritual world, the mystical body; we feel ourselves identified with, and under the doom of, the forces of Evil. Hence the idea of atonement has passed over from the lower or magical to the moral and spiritual religions. In both, man feels guilt and sin, and needs a means of recovering the lost friendship of the gods; or of being restored to the communion of the spiritual order.

Atonement belongs to spirit as such. The Spirit's purpose and aim is universal and not private. Its present life is a war against the internal discords of the world; against sin and sorrow; against the inevitable limitations of the finite and transitory. It is in the world as a healing, harmonising power. All who yield themselves to it are, so far, one and the same; they live a common life and serve a common end. They are members of one mystical body, manifestations of one transcendental life. The Spirit seeks to draw all men to itself; it invites their voluntary adhesion; it is ever soliciting them through their conscience. But when, by sin, they tear themselves from the Eternal to cling to the transitory and corruptible, they become spiritually dead and unable to respond to the inward voice, which grows feebler with every moment of alienation. It is impossible not to feel that those who are nearer to the Spirit acquire some authority and power in the transcendental order: "Whose soever sins ye forgive they are forgiven unto them" was said of the Apostles when they received the Spirit that Jesus had, so to say, earned for them by His death and blood. The Spirit can quicken the Spirit dormant in the sinner, can stimulate the will to a new act of adhesion, can make its reconciliation a matter of experimental certainty. In this sense the sufferings of all the just, united with the central sufferings of One Who, in His own experience and in the faith of Christianity was so closely identified with God, are naturally considered to have an atoning value. Jesus has the plenitude of that magnetism which draws sinners back to God and magnetises them in their turn.

The idea of atonement is a corollary of that of spiritual solidarity; of the mystical body whose members serve one another; of the "communion of saints." The spirit-life is essentially a life of all in each and of each in all. Union with God means union with all that are God's—whether actually or potentially.

Life is a poor and narrow thing if we lose sight of the great principle revealed to us in the doctrine of Christ's atonement.

(*h*) THE PHENOMENAL AND THE SPIRITUAL

If there is, in apocalyptic thought, a sharp dualism between Good and Evil, God and Satan, the Spirit of Light and the Spirit of Darkness, that between Spirit and Matter is far less sharp than in Greek thought or in the Pauline-Johannine writings. The notion of God as the subsistent idea of Being; of the transcendent world as built up of subsistent class notions purified of all content that would determine them to time or place; the conception of spirit as the subject and cause of our abstractions and generalisations and, therefore, as itself something indifferent to matter, time and space—all this metaphysic was as far removed from apocalyptic thought as it is from our own. It belongs to that so-called realism, which were better called idealism in that it regards ideas and abstractions as the ultimate act and reality, as the cause of the concrete, contingent, illusory and potential.

Finding general ideas immutable and indifferent to time and place and content, it endows them with a mysterious eternity and ubiquity, and bids man despise the particular and concrete in his quest of truth and beatitude. It forgets that the divisions and headings, under which the library of our experience is unified and catalogued, are entirely subordinate and ministerial to a knowledge of the contents of the books it contains. These it despises as contingent and mutable; and finds the only worthy object of knowledge in the headings of the catalogue. The categories of the understanding are the reflex of the transcendent and eternal world in the flowing waters of the contingent and material.

The extent to which this conception of the transcendent has influenced later Christian Mysticism, through Alexandrine and Scholastic philosophy, is notorious. As a symbolism of the transcendent order it had, no doubt, some advantages over the simple imaginative visions of the Apocalypse, and was in many ways morally and spiritually fruitful. But in its contempt of the particular and material, in its violent antithesis of matter and spirit, and in the moral corollaries of that antithesis, it was altogether unfortunate. It was in no sense an hypothesis suggested and moulded by spiritual experience, but a thought-out system, imposed upon it. It affected to be a translation of revealed divinity into terms of current philosophy, and to possess actual, and not merely symbolic, truth; while, in fact, it was a translation of one symbolism into another.

Apocalyptic thought knew nothing of these hypostatised abstractions, these animated class-notions. It knew of earthly bodies and spiritual bodies; bodies of flesh and bodies of glory. Its heaven, its angels, its very God, were clothed in bodies of light. Of a disembodied immortality it had no notion. The two orders were not wholly discontinuous; far less were they violently opposed. One language fitted them both.

Here an important truth is safeguarded that is imperilled by the Alexandrine and pseudo-Dionysian symbolism. As M. Le Roy has pointed out, analogy needs three terms in order to arrive at a fourth. If we have no experience whatever of the transcendent, analogy cannot help us. If I had no experience whatever of light, I could learn nothing from the analogy. As a symphony is to a sound, so is a painting to light; I must at least have the rudiments of vision. So, too, I must have the rudiments of the transcendent life in myself if I am to desire an integral knowledge and enjoyment of it, and to figure it to myself in analogies drawn from other orders of experience.

Of this rudimentary transcendence, the light and glory of the apocalyptic vision are a symbol. This world and the other belong to one system, one self-explanatory whole; as do body and soul. They act and re-act. They have a common history to some extent. The visible is patterned in the invisible; the battle on earth is the double of a battle in the skies.

All this symbolism preserves the importance of the interests of the present life and their bearing on eternity; and condemns the aloofness and apathy of abstract spirituality and of that ultimate pessimism which is favoured by a contempt of the material and concrete. It preserves the motive for struggling to make this world what we know it can never be. It assures us (to use a hackneyed quotation) that "life is real, life is earnest," just because "the grave is not its goal."

It is in and through what we call the material order, the world of sensible phenomena, that the spiritual element of our being is brought to consciousness and tries vainly to know and realise itself. It acts on, and is affected by, the sensible. Nor can we conceive it as conscious, out of all relation to the sensible. Have we a right to conclude that, because it is strangled and blinded by its present medium of self-expression, it can express itself without any medium at all? Were not this to fall into the fallacy of abstract and negative spirituality again? We know that each sense opens up to us a new phenomenal order that else had been non-existent for us, and that by it our spirit has been liberated indefinitely. What had it been without the world of colour or of music? What might it not be were other worlds opened to its consciousness? And what probability is there that we are not blind and deaf to a thousand worlds around us? If, then, the only transcendent life we know is thus related to the phenomenal, what right have we to assume that the satisfaction it seeks means a release from, and not a fuller embodiment in, the phenomenal; or that the transcendent order involves the negation, and not the completion, of the phenomenal? Empty spirit of all relation to the phenomenal, and what is left but a word? And does not the phenomenal enter, however vaguely, into the essence of that life whose rudiments we experience now, but whose expansion and satisfaction we know is impossible within the limited potentialities of that fraction of the phenomenal world which is revealed to us by our five poor senses? I own that I cannot find in myself any longing to escape from all that is beautiful and wonderful in physical nature, or in human life and interests, but rather a desire to enjoy a great deal more of the same without its now inevitable limitations; nor could I be consoled by the contemplation of subsistent classnotions, ranged harmoniously under that of allembracing entity. I feel sure that the apocalyptic Heaven, with all its colour and music, and light and happiness, is a truer symbol of man's spiritual aspirations than the cold constructions of intellectualism, in that it escapes a false antithesis of the spiritual and the phenomenal, and recognises the one as an inseparable correlative of the other. The transcendent is not the spiritual as opposed to the phenomenal; but the whole as opposed to an infinitesimal fraction of possible spiritual experience. Our spirit-life, our disinterested love of the universal Good, our unqualified worship of the Right in conduct, thought and feeling, is just the life of the Whole that is immanent in every part; that seeks its own universal end primarily and that of the part inclusively; that can never be satisfied by what is an end only relatively to the part, but clamours for the universal and eternal Good. Our mind is the mind of a part, not of the Whole. It is built for the service of our temporal life and immediate ends, and can never comprehend the spirit and its universal end; yet it possesses a fractional knowledge of the transcendent, which it can perfect by analogies derived from its own narrow field of phenomena.

Incarnation, embodied immortality, sacraments, external worship, a visible Church; all are founded on this correlativity of the spiritual and phenomenal; on the idea that the spiritual utters itself in, and is addressed through, the phenomenal; that they are as inseparable as subject and object; that pure spirit is a pure abstraction. As our mind is tied for its categories to that small part of the phenomenal field to which our bodies belong, it has no proper idea of the transcendent Whole and its relations, nor can it determine how the spirit in each of us is related to the universality of Spirit. But judged by the test of life and fruitfulness, the symbolism of apocalyptic imagery is truer to our spiritual needs than that of Hellenic intellectualism.

XIII

THE APOCALYPTIC VISION AND THE CATHOLIC CHURCH

ENOUGH has been said, then, to show that the religious "idea" of Jesus, embodied in apocalyptic imagery, possesses an abiding value, in no way dependent on the literal worth of that imagery. A true revelation of the whole in terms of an infinitesimal part, of the transcendent in terms of present experience, is not possible. Yet the Whole, the spiritual, lives in us and moves us toward a universal End or Good, that exists for the consciousness of the Whole and not for that of the part. So far as we are freely to accept and co-operate with the instinct of the Spirit, we must have, at least, some symbolic notion of its nature and end; some fiction explanatory of the movements that we experience within ourselves—a fiction suggested by them; verified and criticised by its success in intensifying and enriching our spirituality. Such visions and revelations command our faith by their liberating appeal to our spiritual need, spirit answering to spirit. They explain us to ourselves; they set free the springs of life. Such was and such is the power of the Gospel of Jesus. It was a vision of the transcendent that fixed a manner of feeling and living whose fruitfulness was simply a matter of experience. It was a *schema*, a way of taking things, as true to ultimate reality as any expression of the Whole in terms of so small a part can be. It had the practical truth of a correct guide to our present religious experience; and, as the spontaneous creation of His own experience, working with the religious language and categories of His time and tradition, it had the representative value of an analogy.

Obviously there is no universal language, and the Gospel Idea had to incarnate itself in that of a particular time and place. But concrete imagery is of more universal significance than conceptual language; the doctrine of repentance is less generally understandable than the story of the prodigal son. For universal and abiding symbolism an apocalyptic vision is far less corruptible than a theology. Moreover, the Idea symbolised is one of universal validity and within the spiritual experience of all. For these reasons the contingency and particularity of Gospel language and imagery detract but slightly from its permanent and universal value for humanity.

It embodies and evokes a development of the religious Idea that cannot be outgrown till men have outgrown Christ.

It is a Gospel for the poor and afflicted, who, under the discipline of experience, have ceased to place their hopes in the present life; and for those to whom reflection and observation have revealed the iron law of failure and mortality, which dissipates the dream of salvation by progress. It stands or falls with faith in another life, in which the stifled spirit can realise itself in another order of experience. It is religion primarily and explicitly; it is morality inclusively, because morality is an exercise of the spiritual life under contingencies peculiar to our present partial experience. "But when that which is perfect is come, that which is in part shall be done away." When the work is finished, labour ceases; weary man enters into his rest.

By faith man walks consciously in the light of eternity, and sees earth and its burden as from a distant planet—a speck in immensity. And yet he labours for the alleviation of its sorrows as they can never labour who need the assurance of success. The dulness of the most ordinary toil, the bitterness of the hardest lot, is illuminated by the consciousness of its transcendent significance. Translate the Gospel vision into merely ethical values; tell us that eternal life is moral life, and the Kingdom of Heaven the eventual triumph of social reform; and lo! the gourd whose leaves have so long shaded mankind from the sickening heat of the desert is withered down to the roots.

When we compare the religious idea of Jesus, as it emerges from the most drastic and impartial criticism of the Gospels, with that of the Catholic Church; when we consider the type of spirituality exhibited in her saints, canonised or uncanonised; when we listen to her classical preachers and study her ascetical tradition; it is impossible to deny that she has been true, not only to the religious idea of her Founder, but to the very form of its expression. Nay, her fidelity to the letter; her unwillingness to tamper with what has been the vehicle and sacrament of much spiritual life and experience; her refusal to admit the symbolic character of the apocalyptic vision; her determination to treat it as revealed truth of the phenomenal order and make it a criterion of history and science—all this has gradually weakened her influence and brought her into conflict with the modern mind.

Yet, in this again, she is only blindly faithful to the past. The distinction she ignores is one that has slowly been forced upon us by our growing knowledge of the laws of the human mind.

Its recognition in earlier centuries would have been miraculous. To refuse any longer to recognise it, is to imperil the Christian religion; and this perhaps is the main contention of the Catholic Modernist. He certainly does not desire to substitute any conceptual translation of that vision for the vision itself. He knows that any translation of the kind would still be a symbolism. He feels that the original self-embodiment of Christ's Idea is a work of Divine inspiration, and preserves it for us more truthfully than can any rendering of it. But he would have its symbolic character explicitly recognised, and its meaning rendered by each age in its own terms.

From all that has been said it is easy to see the difference between the real development of an idea and the logical development of premisses. An idea, like Religion or Christianity, presents itself to consciousness first as a dull craving, or a blind instinct making for an end, that is yet unknown, but is progressively revealed as the instinct tries to understand and realise itself. Thus the idea of the End, to which instinct drives us, comes gradually to consciousness by a process of development. In all stages of its embodiment it is the same idea that is manifested under some aspect or another. The criterion of these developments cannot be the idea itself, which is only slowly coming to consciousness and can never be apprehended exhaustively. It can only be the satisfaction or dissatisfaction of that need to which the idea corresponds. Thus we do not criticise a civilisation by some celestial archetype, but by the expansion and enrichment of life; not by its nearness to the unknown End at which it aims, but by its distance from its point of departure.

Hence, in regard to whatever additions or subtractions the revelation of Jesus may have undergone in the course of time, the pertinent point is whether they have corrupted, or have preserved, or even integrated the Idea of the Gospel. Avowedly the aim of the Church's dogmatic labour has been to preserve the original sense of revelation incorrupt. It is to the collective memory of the whole body that its guardianship has been committed. But memory needs criticism and correction, and this it receives from the understanding. In the measure that symbols were taken literally theology was at war with reason when reason, excluding the literal acceptance of apocalyptic imagery, seemed hostile to faith. In the defence of positions that were rationally impossible, and yet were confirmed by religious experience as revealed truth, many untenable conclusions must have seemed bound up with the faith. The story of the conflict between Scripture and science abounds with instances. It seemed a conflict between internal and external experience; between fact and fact. We blame the Church of the seventeenth century for not possessing the criticism of the twentieth. We might more justly blame the Church of the twentieth for abiding by that of the seventeenth. Errors of this kind were the result, not of a departure from, but of an ill-judged fidelity to revelation. The light of truth shone through the distorting medium of a perverse understanding. Besides these protective errors there were various protective truths which, without belonging to the original revelation, were necessary to secure the freshness of its features and colours against the smoke and dust of time; and these can in no sense be regarded as corruptions any more than the explanatory ritual that surrounds the simple essential rite of baptism, and is merely a development of the idea of baptism.

Finally, it is the very nature of the human mind to integrate, in the language of fiction and imagination, the ideas and ideals that are suggested to it in the language of fact. These fictions are not true to the fact on which they are founded, but are true to the idea suggested by those facts—truer than fact, in their deeper sense. There have been, no doubt, many such spontaneous and unconscious integrations of the apocalyptic presentment of the transcendent order, and, like the Apocalypse itself, they have been inserted in the series of external phenomena. But the sole pertinent question is, not their phenomenal, but their spiritual, truth, except where it can be shown that their spiritual value depends, as it sometimes does, on their historicity. In other cases they belong to the category of visions embodying inward experiences, and reconstructing the world and history according to the exigencies of the spirit.

Notwithstanding, and partly because of, these developments and alterations, it is impossible to deny that the revelation of the Catholic religion and that of Jesus are the same, not only in substance but largely in form. I must go further and say that, far from feeling more at home to-day among Liberal Protestants than among orthodox Roman Catholics, the Jesus of the first century would be in sympathy with just those elements of Catholicism that are least congenial to the modern mind—not to say the mind of Modernists—not only with the transcendental, but with the literal, value of the Catholic presentment of the transcendental; with sacraments, temples, priests and altars; with miracles, diabolic possessions and exorcisms; with devils and angels and all the supernaturalism of His own age and tradition. For all these things He had no word, no thought of censure; but only for their abuse and exploitation; for their perversion to unspiritual and immoral ends by priests and people. Against superstition as an error of the intellect He has little, if anything, to say in the way of warning. His zeal is not against the letter but against a literalism that destroys the spirit to which it should minister; that forgets the end in the means; that substitutes outward observance for moral and spiritual sacrifice. He does not condemn the lighter matters of the law, but the neglect of the weightier. He repudiates the traditions of men only so far as they make vain the tradition of Moses, and, for Him, that tradition justified the substance of the Jewish religion. It was in the forms of such a tradition that He necessarily embodied His Gospel, and the Catholic Church has preserved the earthen vessel with its heavenly treasure; while those who have broken and cast away the vessel seem to have lost much of the treasure. Ought we not still to keep it while carefully distinguishing it from its content?

.   .   .   .   .   .

In all this I am thinking of the Catholic religion, not as a theological system on paper, nor as an institution governed by a hierarchy in other than spiritual interests; but as a personal religion lived

by what must always be a small minority of
professed Catholics. I am thinking of what it
does and has done for the souls of those who not
merely profess it, but believe in it, and use it.
I am thinking of the bird free on the wing, not
crushed and crumpled in the grip of the hawk;
of the Church living, not of the Church dying and
dead. Religion has ever been exploited by priests
and politicians, who see in it a means of gripping
men by what is deepest in them—their conscience;
and so controlling their lives, their services, their
fortunes, to their own selfish and ambitious ends.
They run it as business men, void of all artistic
sympathy, might run a theatre, employing the best
actors or the worst as may prove more profitable.
In religion itself they have no sort of interest—
only in its serviceableness to their own non-religious
interests. They favour laxity or sanctity according to their market value, and, as a rule, it pays
better to cater for the groundlings than for the
elect few. No religion of any duration or influence
has escaped this degradation and corruption. Few
have had the misfortune to be exploited on so
large a scale by their own guardians. Yet, in spite
of this misfortune, the Roman Catholic religion
still lives in the grip of the hawk.

Whether it has strength enough to escape, who
can tell? Dead or alive, its claim to be the

authentic tradition of Christianity seems to me to be incontestable. Judge, then, what truth there is in the popular idea that Modernism is a Protestantising movement in the Roman Church, converging to the same point as Liberal Protestantism.

But a larger problem is suggested by the comparative study of religions. If Catholicism be authentic Christianity, how does Christianity stand in relation to other religions?

PART II
CHRISTIANITY AND RELIGION

I

EXCLUSIVENESS AND INTOLERANCE

IN earlier stages of civilisation the rivalry and mutual exclusiveness of religions was more frankly a form of *esprit de corps*. It did not cover itself under the pretext of the unity of God, of Truth, of Righteousness. It was little more than another aspect of the rivalry of clans, tribes and peoples. Israel's God was a God above all gods. The gods of her neighbours were devils. The enmities of earth had their counterparts in heaven. The egotism, exclusiveness and ambition of the people were embodied in and sanctified by its god or gods. When neighbours were peaceful and allied, they easily practised more than one religion. It was well to be at peace with as many gods as possible.

But this liberalism was usually discouraged by priests, who had no wish to divide the honours and emoluments of their profession and, therefore, presented their own god as a jealous god. They dared not say "There *is* no other god," but only "Thou shalt have no other god." They preached monolatry, but not monotheism. The idea of a supreme God, of a Father and great King above all gods, was not far; and the denial of godhead to all the rest, who then became angels or devils, was bound to follow. Yet even such a God was rather a power in nature, a principal part, than something above and before all worlds. He was a postulate of man's practical needs, rather than of his philosophical search for a first and universal cause.

Not till religion passed from its magical stage; not till its regalia were transferred to the worship of spirit and truth and righteousness, was monotheism firmly established on its proper basis. Truth is one, absolute, exclusive. To worship any other god is not merely rebellion and desertion; it is folly, immorality, falsehood. There can be but one religion and one only; all the rest are false. There can be no toleration for falsehood and immorality; exclusiveness is a duty.

The rivalries of monotheistic and spiritual religions are not concerned with *what* we shall worship, but with *how*—whether at Jerusalem or in this mountain. Each stands for certain ideas of truth and goodness; certain conceptions of God and His Will. If these are right, all others must be wrong; for truth is one. Intolerance and exclusiveness are thus deepened. They pass from the surface affections down to the very roots of conscience.

It cannot be otherwise if the truth about God and His Will be as ascertainable and as certain as, or more certain than, the truth about the laws of physical phenomena. What is more exclusive than science? what more intolerant than geometry? And seeing how intimate is the bearing of truth on life and happiness, is not the liberty of disseminating a false religion far more reprehensible than that of vending and advertising deleterious foods or medicines? Hence every religion that believes itself to possess the truth about God and His Will must be exclusive and intolerant. What underlies this intolerance is the conviction that truth is one and that religious truth is supremely important; and, with this, the more doubtful assumption that we possess it and others do not. Given this assumption, tolerance is simply immorality. It has been the assumption of Jew, Moslem and Christian, and is the secret of their exclusiveness. It is the assumption of every sect of Christianity as against every other sect. In the measure that the Christian Apocalypse has been translated from imaginative into intellectual language—into concepts and theological statements—and has been brought into one body with the whole of our systematised knowledge, intolerance itself has become more systematic.

We notice this tendency even in the Johannine and Pauline writings, with their theological preoccupations. But it would be a mistake to view this intolerance as a pure accretion and not as, in some sense, a development of the synoptic teaching. Christ did not impose theological dogmas under pain of eternal damnation; but He imposed the Apocalypse of the Kingdom of Heaven, of which theology is the intellectual rendering, under pain of that condemnation. Of the Gospel in its apocalyptical form He says: "He that believeth not shall be damned." He only shall be saved who, believing that the End is near, is baptised unto repentance and a new life. The text is dubious; but it epitomises the whole of the synoptic teaching. For Jesus, salvation was of the Jews. If many should come from the East and the West, it was to Jewry they were to come; it was with Abraham, Isaac and Jacob they were to sit at meat in the Kingdom. If He preferred many a Gentile and Samaritan to many a soulless Jew, He did not prefer their religion, but their greater worthiness of the Jew's neglected privileges and graces. His was the attitude of the reasonable Roman Catholic to the heretic in good faith and "invincible ignorance."

What He looked to was the ingathering of all these into the one fold of Israel, under Himself as the universal Shepherd. His immediate mission, however, was only to the lost sheep of the house of Israel. Ere the Apostles had preached the Kingdom in all the cities of Israel, the End would come and Gentiles in good faith would be gathered in by the angels from the four quarters of the earth, to be saved in union with the elect of Israel. If we have here the seed of Pauline universalism, we have it in a form consistent with the Catholic tradition of exclusiveness. "Catholic" and "exclusive," far from contradicting, complement one another. Science is catholic and exclusive for the same reason—its objective truth. Because Catholicism is the one and only religion it is the religion for all. If the outsider "in good faith" is saved, it is only because he is on his way to the Church.

When Judaism refused to accept Jesus as the Messiah, we may be sure that the Christian Jews did not regard themselves as seceders; but as the authentic remnant from which the main body had apostatised. What did numbers matter? Had they not Christ the Head? Those who excommunicated the Head had but excommunicated themselves. Christian Israel was the one true Israel, out of which there was no salvation.

Thus, when the smaller West separated from the then far larger East, the West, as possessing the head (i.e. Rome), considered the East schismatic.

Subsequently, when S. Paul found the formalities of the law an obstacle to the ingathering of the Gentiles, he saw that the Gospel and the Spirit were alone essential; that form and observance were free; that the true Israel could accommodate itself in such matters to the habits and customs of its proselytes; could change its outward expression and embodiment of religion to any extent. Yet this widening of the borders did not abolish borders, nor abolish the principle of exclusiveness in any way.

And the same exclusiveness has been the mark of Catholic Christianity at all times: "Outside the Church there is no salvation." An exception has always been made for cases of "good faith," even by the most bigoted, who are loth to admit the frequency of such cases.

But this is no real exception; for the man in good faith is one who is groping his way to the Church. Never is it allowed that he can be saved by his religion, but only in spite of it. Every religion but one is the work of the devil, a snare, an imposture, a spurious imitation, a greater lie in that it embodies and perverts a greater measure of truth. A heretic is worse than an infidel.

II

THE UNIFICATION OF RELIGION

DETESTABLE as this exclusiveness has been in its historical manifestations, we must respect its assertion of the unity and sovereign claims of truth. The sects and heresies of earlier times were as exclusive as the great Church, as willing to persecute when they were able. We are too apt to consider that the oppressed are opposed to the *principle* of oppression. The comparatively modern toleration of other religions is, to a large extent, due to the scepticism suggested by the multiplication of sects, each claiming to be the one authentic Christianity; and by an increased experience of other religions making the same claims as the Christian Church. This scepticism has been systematically deepened by the comparative study of religion, and by all the causes that have brought dogma into disrepute. Truth may be intolerant, but opinion has no business to be so; and religion is felt more and more to be a matter of opinion.

This sort of indifferentism is, however, governed

by the old theological idea of religious truth.
Diverse symbolisms, like diverse rituals, might
stand for the same sense and meaning and be
no more than differences of language. But it
religions are identical with their theological expression, it is plain that not more than one can
be true; and it is infinitely probable that all are
more or less false. Hence a tendency to search
for some one or two truths in which all religions
agree, and to make this the essence of religion,
regarding all the rest, not as development, but as
mere accretion; and to seek a sort of negative
Catholicism by levelling down all these differences
and by emptying the religious idea of all but its
vaguest and most rudimentary content. Christians
are to unite on the basis of the Fatherhood of
God and the Brotherhood of man. All religions
agree that there is a transcendent to which we
should adjust our lives. The nature of that
transcendent, and of our adjustment to it, is
a matter of opinion.

This, of course, is to go back to the germ and
to deny all truth-value to its developments; to
declare the historical religious process mere waste.
It is Rousseau's remedy of a return to savagery,
to the peace of the desert. Indeed, it is not
possible to void the religious form or idea of all
content and determination. About even the

simplest formula and most universal affirmation, agreement can be only verbal. All we can arrive at is a minimum of disagreement. Fatherhood and brotherhood are not abstract mathematical conceptions. The rights, duties and sentiments of paternity are endlessly disputable. The transcendent does not consist merely of transcendence, which is but a relation and attribute of something whose nature is, likewise, endlessly disputable. The term "religiosity," which is coming into vogue to express the "one thing needful" that remains when religions have been purified of all doctrinal and institutional accretions, stands for a mere sentiment, for the sense of an unsatisfied need. Religion is thus reduced to the religious need. Every response to that need is an impertinence. We are to ask, seek and knock, but never to find, receive or enter. We are to feel the significance of life; we must not dare to say what it signifies. Thus the religious idea is condemned to sterility. It is to produce nothing. The moment a green shoot appears, it is to be shorn close to the ground.

Yet this conclusion is almost inevitable if the expression of religion be taken as literal and scientific truth. When it is taken otherwise, namely as symbolic and analogical truth, we are met by another sort of indifferentism. One re-

ligion is as good, instead of as bad, as another.
Each says the same thing in its own way—the
way best suited for its time and place. But this
view, again, denies any sort of variation and development of the religious idea corresponding to these
varieties of its expression. We might as well say
that, because the idea of life is expressed in every
living species, one species is as good as another,
and that man has no advantage over a mushroom; or that, because the idea of civilisation is
expressed in the lowest as in the highest forms,
these have no advantage over those. Plainly the
idea and its embodiment act and re-act. It is,
doubtless, the whole idea of life that seeks expression in each species; but its success is only
fractional, and limited by the material it works in.
It is revealed far more fully in some forms
than in others; in all, than in any one. We call
man a microcosm, for he reveals life more fully
and variously than any one creature we know.
But he is a poor compendium of the total manifestation of life given us in the living world. And,
similarly, the religious idea reveals itself more
fully in some religions than in others; but in all,
more than in any one.

When this is recognised we are naturally
tempted to a sort of syncretic Catholicism, embracing all religions as one integral expression of

the religious idea. We might as well try to live the life of all living species at once. A logical union of genus or species is not a real union. As the branches of the tree of life bifurcate and diverge, they grow more characterised and unlike one another. So of the varieties of the religious idea. They do not converge towards, but diverge from, a point of sameness. Schism is their very law. So far as they are alive and vigorous, each pushes forward in its own direction and away from others; reunion becomes less and less possible. The tendency towards reunion among the Christian sects of to-day is the result of weariness and decay; of scepticism as to the value of their several systems. The withered branches break off at their point of bifurcation. Union is restored by going backwards to an original state of indetermination.

If the laws of life are any guide to the laws of religion, we must expect to find that, in spite of their parentage or cousinship, the relation between different religions is that of rivalry and hostility, and that there is more reason for such rivalry in the more nearly allied branches of the family. I speak of spiritual religions, each with its implicit or explicit claim to be the one and only religion, intolerant of all the rest. Among them the law of competition prevails and stimulates development. The victory is plainly with the most elastic and pliable; with the most catholic. An ideally catholic religion would eliminate all rivals. As it is, we have, side by side with legions of short-lived sects and cults that come and go like leaves, a few which are catholic enough to have held millions of men together for many centuries. It was to its extraordinary plasticity that Christianity owed its conquest over the senile and ossified religions of its day; and the same holds good of all the great religions. If a truly catholic religion is ever to be realised, it will not be by a sinking of differences and an insistence on the sole importance of the generic idea or starting-point of all divergences; nor by an impossible unification of essentially incompatible systems, as though they were members of one organism. For each system is whole and rounded off; each is an attempt to express the *whole* idea and not merely a part of it; none demands another as its complement and explanation.

It is, however, abstractly conceivable that some one system should be related to the rest as is man to other terrestrial species; that it should comprehend nearly all their principal advantages and surpass them in other respects beyond comparison; that it should be so evidently a deeper and fuller expression of religion as to become, first, the principal, and, at last, the only religion in the world. And this might happen either by the rise of a new religion or by the development of an old one. Such a catholicism would, therefore, be the result, not of any sort of reunion, or cessation of inevitable rivalry, but of a world-old conflict, ending in the survival of the fittest.

Looking back on the history of religion, nothing is more improbable. If induction be worth anything, we may be sure that things will be as they have always been, and that dissension will ever be the law of the religious world.

Yet we cannot deny that new factors, new situations, may interfere to modify the uniformities of the past. All our laws suppose constant conditions; but we live now under many conditions that did not obtain in earlier times. Nations, continents and the whole world are drawn closer together than ever before by commerce, by means of communication, by scientific truth. All former civilisations perished; but ours can hardly perish. It is too widespread, too amply and deeply recorded, to be more than locally obliterated. Its utilities are too manifold and evident to be abandoned. If it perished in Europe it would live on in America, and spread thence over the whole world. No former civilisation had any such position of vantage. It is abstractly conceivable that the history of religions might have a similar ending; that some one religion might at last prevail and abide.

What has given our civilisation its advantage and promise of duration is its grasp of the laws of nature and of life. Our control of nature depends upon our understanding of her uniformities, on our ability to anticipate experience, to be prepared against surprise. Truth is just the correct anticipation of experience. In every civilisation man seeks a passage to a wide ocean of free untrammelled life for all. But heretofore his way has ever been blocked at the last. Now he seems to have found the main. Heaven knows he has not found bliss; but, at most, freedom to search for alleviations of his misery. Discoveries, like speech, writing, printing, steam, electricity, are acquisitions for everywhere and for ever; and our civilisation rests on a whole multitude of these discoveries. Man's life, his pleasures and pains, are, henceforth and for ever, on a larger and swiftly growing scale—one that bids fair to exhaust his nervous capacity and hasten his extinction, since he cannot turn back.

May we not then conjecture that a relatively universal and permanent religion would be one that rested on a knowledge of the laws and uniformities revealed by a comparative study of religions and a study of religious psychology? that it would be, in some reserved sense, a scientific religion? Catholicism is the characteristic of science as it is of truth. Science is not local but cosmopolitan—the same for the American, the Hindu, the Hottentot.

Now we know that the eighteenth century witnessed an attempt to rationalise religion and render it independent of faith and revelation; to substitute so-called natural for supernatural theology; to show that the existence of one God and the immortality of the soul were dictates of human reason and, as such, formed the substance of universal religion. This idea was, no doubt, a legacy of scholastic theology, purified of its revealed elements. It took no account of the history of religions; made no study of specifically religious experience. It was the *a priori* construction of a philosophical intellectualism, that is now practically obsolete. If "scientific" means suggested and controlled by experience, nothing could be less "scientific" than the religion of the Encyclopædists; nothing less Catholic than the philosophy on which it was built. It was just scholastic theodicy with the supernatural omitted. Hence its marble coldness, its inability to make any sort of appeal to religious feeling. It had not sprung from the heart and could not speak to the heart. In England it produced an Evangelical and Catholic reaction; from rational theology and rational ethics men sought warmth and colour and life in sentimentalism, mysticism, sacramentalism.

It is easy for us now to see how this rationalising attempt failed and must have failed; but we should respect its attempt to discover a religion that should be Catholic and true for all men alike and at all times. The attempt failed because it was thoroughly unscientific, based on a metaphysic spun out of an analysis of concepts, and not suggested and controlled at every step by experience. It took no account of any religion but Christianity, and it treated Christianity as a theology not as a life.

Since then the historical and comparative method has asserted and proved its value, and, together with a practically new psychology, has rendered possible a true science of religious phenomena. Enough has been done to assure us that much more can be done to understand the uniformities that control this department of individual and collective life, and to determine what is normal and what abnormal, what is progressive and what decadent. If an analogous knowledge enables us to diagnose and cure the ailments of the body or the ills of society, may we not hope to remedy those of religion? We can no more create religion than we can create life, or by taking thought add one cubit to our stature. But we can condition the creation, growth and health of the body, and, in other matters than religion, we can condition the growth of the soul—in both cases through a better and more scientific understanding of nature's uniformities. Why, then, should it be a profanity to suggest that science may, in like manner, come to the aid of religion? Is not science from God and for God?

If we trace from its origin the history of certain tracts and departments of human experience that are now fertilised and regulated by their corresponding sciences, we shall find that, after long centuries of confusion and groping, they have, at last, been rationalised by some discovery or fertilising hypothesis, which has given them objective and universal validity. In their chaotic, pre-scientific stage their characteristics have been just those of religion, as we see it now all round us.

Though it is yet far from exactitude and universal validity, the art and science of Medicine offers the closest parallel to religion in many ways, as dealing with a general and permanent need of humanity. In its pre-scientific stage it is absolutely chaotic in its diagnoses and prescriptions—a wilderness of fables and superstitions, as various as the vagaries of the human imagination. There is at most the unity, so to speak, of its idea. It looks to that adjustment which we call health; it seeks the causes and cures of disease; it professes to proceed experimentally or empirically; it justifies itself by its fruitfulness. But it has no idea of what experiment really means, or of the conditions of a valid induction. It imputes ailments to mystical or purely fanciful causes, on the grounds of some merely subjective association of ideas. In the same way it devises fanciful cures, that may often cure by mere suggestion. Herbs that resemble a part of the body are good for that part. A disease is a devil that must be exorcised; an emetic throws him out, and, if the emetic be beneficial, it is because the devil has departed. Obviously this sort of ætiology will not hold good for any two tribes, let alone for the whole world. The progress of thought consists in gradually separating the series of objective, and universally valid, from that of subjective, experiences. In the measure that their confusion prevails, man is, to all intents and purposes, mad; and it is this note of insanity that characterises medicine and religion in their early stages. Dreams and reality are mixed up; subjective connections are objectified.

For the simple needs of an almost animal life imaginative associations are practically enough, without any attempt at systematic understanding and logical inference. But understanding is there, untrained and unskilled, interfering with purely animal psychology, and producing the wildest confusion in its clumsy quest of order, as we see in the whole history of magic, tokens and taboos. It is already beginning to separate subjective from objective, and to search for that truth of which the animal imagination has no need. Not till man seeks to distinguish subjective from objective, does he fall into the madness of confounding one with the other. Yet it is from this ever-flowing stream of wild hypotheses and conjectures that useful, and objectively valid, discoveries are selected.

In *Psyche's Task* J. G. Frazer shows how government, marriage and the right of property were products of delirium, justified later by their unsuspected social utility. Chance has had much to do with our greatest inventions. The inventive man is one with a rich imagination and active intelligence, who makes ten thousand hypotheses, of which some one or two are bound to be fruitful.

If, then, mental progress consists in the cultivation of tracts of reason in a boundless wilderness of delirium, it need not surprise us that man's earlier efforts, compared with our own attainments, should seem capricious, fanciful and incoherent. Even to-day the diversities of medical opinion and practice are enough to show that the science is yet far removed from unification and general validity. But we now recognise the need and possibility of this unification, and we know the methods by which it can be continually approached. The complexity of the subject-matter, together with the conservatism of patients and practitioners, offer an obstruction from which astronomy, chemistry, electricity and such sciences are free. But already Medicine has passed from its chaotic and subjective to its objective and rational stage; and its catholicism is in view.

Again, in early Medicine, personal authority exercises an exaggerated influence and takes the place of intrinsic arguments. Schools centre round names rather than round systems or theories. Even so late as in Burton's *Anatomy of Melancholy* we see the enormous part played by faith, by the authority of great names. A dogma is just the *ipse dixit* of a great teacher; it is imposed in the name of his prestige. To question it were insolence. No one questions the educational and manuductory value of such dogmatism within due limits. Pass those limits and it becomes a hindrance. The arrogance of doctors and teachers has been one of the greatest obstacles to human progress; few men can withstand the corrupting influence of unlimited trust. Credulity in the listeners breeds untruthfulness in the speaker. A good deal of our truthfulness is due to the fear of being found out and losing our credit. When travelling was rare, a traveller's tale or a sailor's yarn was synonymous with a tissue of exaggerations and inventions. The teacher who professes to draw his information from sources inaccessible to his public, such as private revelations or special faculties of divination, or from regions visited by himself alone, will be more than human if he do not grow indifferent to truth; if he do not state as probable what is only possible, and as certain what is only probable; if he do not bolster up loose with still looser assertions. There is something worse than deliberate lying, and that is the habit of gratuitous assertion; of saying, not what we know to be untrue, but what we do not know to be true. Nine-tenths of our untruthfulness is of this sort; and it is fostered by the credulity or the indifference of our hearers.

Both truth and truthfulness are late social developments, and suppose a clear idea of the difference between the subjective and the objective series of phenomena. Primitive men, like very young children, are hardly capable of formal and conscious lying. They give out, as of equal value, what they have seen and what they have imagined. And in some measure the savage survives in us all.

When men are trusted without limit, when they profess to draw their knowledge from esoteric sources, when their inaccuracies cannot be checked or their information verified, when, in short, they are placed in primitive conditions, their primitive nature comes out, and the whole weight of their authority is lent to the obstruction of truth and the multiplication of error.

Not till men are drawn together from all quarters to compare notes is their trust in personal authority shaken by the hopeless inconsistency of its utterances. Not till medicine and other sciences passed from the sway of personal authority, and began to draw their knowledge from sources accessible to all; not till their professors were exposed to criticism and detection, did those sciences become unified, objective and catholic.

III

THE SCIENCE OF RELIGIONS

OUR experience in the realm of profane science has given us an ideal of unification and catholicism. We cannot help desiring that religion should be redeemed from chaos to order; that so universal a need should be met with an universally valid response. In medicine we do not look for a panacea for all diseases, each disease has its own remedy. But we look for a science that shall govern the diagnosis and remedy of every disease; and that science must be one and universal. In the same way we feel that religion should be one, but we have not got beyond the desire for unity. Religion is still multitudinous, chaotic and capricious; still mainly under the sway of personal authority. We are only gathering the materials for an induction, and hazarding vague and premature hypotheses. The subject-matter is complex, not only on account of its vastness but by reason of its subtlety. We can get at the structure and workings of the body with our senses and instruments; not at those of the soul. What is deepest in our nature is last to be unearthed. Psychology and metaphysic are the most backward of sciences; man has ever been curious about them, but his curiosity has been futile. Again, man's affections and interests interfere with freedom of religious inquiry as with no other matter. Religion usually claims supernatural authority. Its gods are jealous gods; its priests, jealous priests. It is rooted in the customs, traditions, fears and hopes of the people. In its spiritual and moral phase it becomes exclusive on principle, and each form claims the universality and perpetuity of truth and justice. Moreover, those whose personal religious experiences have been associated with a given system cling to that system *en bloc*, neither distinguishing occasions from causes, nor the causative element from other elements of the system. If a mixture A.B.C.D. has cured them, they will have nothing to do with D.E.F.G., though D. may have been just the one element that mattered. Hence they cling to the whole system in the name of conscience and personal religious experience. It is not wonderful, then, that the unification of religion should seem the remotest and least probable of contingencies.

Yet what brings it within the field of the possible is the growing recognition of the universality and perpetuity of man's religious need and of his effort to satisfy it ; of an important tract of normal experience that has not yet been brought into order with the rest of man's experience and that, in its wild state, is as fruitful of evil as, were it cultivated, it might be of good.

The notion that religion is a disease of man's intellectual childhood, something that he throws off with his bibs and tuckers, is being rapidly discredited. It still governs some of the leaders in the new science of religions, who are hasty to generalise, instead of collecting the materials and perfecting the methods of a successful induction. According to them, the end of such a science is to prove religions a delusion. It is rather a history of follies and fallacies, whose practical end is to deliver us from so disastrous a superstition. This view is, no doubt, favoured by the obvious aspect of primitive religions, and by the survival of their forms and categories in later religions, down to the present time. It was ghost-worship at the beginning, it must be a disguised ghost-worship at the end. The stream cannot rise above its source.

This might be more plausible did we not distinguish between magical religion on the one hand and moral and spiritual religion on the other. What is continuous, is the form, not the substance. Magical religion is the ancestor of science; shall we say, therefore, that science is but disguised magic? Man's earliest gods were but the powers of nature conceived personally, which man strove to manage in the interests of his temporal life, and sometimes of its prolongation in the post-mortem world of dreams. The ancestry of spiritual religion is to be sought in the beginnings of man's moral sense. When he comes to recognise Righteousness as the supreme power and law of the universe and of his own life, he strips his idols bare, and transfers the paraphernalia of religious worship to that supreme spiritual power. On the other hand, his growing interpretation of nature dispenses gradually with personified agencies, and science emerges from its religious wrappings. Thus the two streams of development cross one another and, at the point of intersection, morality steps into the clothes of magical religion and science steps out of them. This, of course, is a logical schematisation but, in the rough, it corresponds to history.

Religion then, in its magical stage, stood for the beginnings of man's scientific effort, his search for the knowledge and control of the phenomena of nature. In its spiritual stage it stands for a development of his moral effort and an expansion of his whole spiritual interest—moral, intellectual and affective,—of his supra-individual and universal selfhood. The study of religions is, therefore, not a study of illusions, but of the process by which truth struggles through darkness into light. No doubt magical religion belongs to man's childhood and must be discarded in his maturity. But we do ill to treat it as delirium. It was the lowly beginning of something great. The embryo of a man is grotesque and at first not distinguishable outwardly from that of a rabbit, but, judged by what comes out of it, it has an immeasurable interest and worth.

Again, spiritual religion, far from being outgrown like a toy, becomes more and more of an exigency with the deepening of man's moral and spiritual life and of his inevitable discontent with what this life offers or can ever possibly offer. He wants something different in kind, an imperishable bread. This want is dulled by his engrossment in the rush of material progress; but obtrudes itself with the growth of his moral ideals and his sense of their unattainableness. Man's spiritual and moral growth leads straight to a pessimism that only religion can cure. Spiritual religion is a demand of his age and grey hairs, not of his babyhood.

The science of religion, therefore, has for its object, not ravings and rubbish, but the highest life of man's soul; his quest for the true, the good and the fair, and for God Who is their synthesis. It can no more create such life than medicine can create that of the body; but it can determine its laws, condition its fertility, and criticise its developments to a great extent. It can discover the unity that underlies its multiplicity. We are far from such a consummation, but we have no reason to despair of it.

Now the unity and catholicity of the science of religions is a very different thing from the unity and catholicity of religion. This, as we have ventured to suggest, can only result from the survival of some one form in virtue of its overwhelming advantages; not from a levelling-down process, nor from a return to a common point of divergence with a cancelling of all the labours of development. If our civilisation has become cosmopolitan and perpetual through its knowledge of the laws of life and nature, a like knowledge of the laws of religious life, social and individual, might give the same overwhelming advantage to some one religion. This would not mean finality, but the right direction of the course of development; the discovery of a free and open road, after many vain excursions up blind alleys. It ought to be possible, from a study of the origin, growth and decay of various religions, to determine the laws of religion in general, to find a criterion and a method by which its life may be indefinitely prolonged and expanded.

Should such a science, in the course of time, shape itself out of the present historical and psychological study of existing and bygone religions, it could not fail to exert a powerful influence on the various living embodiments of the religious idea; of which none could long survive which was known to defy the laws of its life. Civilisations that were unable to adapt themselves to the light of history and science have yielded before those systems that are more intelligent and adaptable, and that tend to become catholic and perpetual. And so with any idea as it comes to be, no longer merely felt and gropingly followed, but clearly understood. The first attempts to understand it result in a half-understanding or misunderstanding, which is often obstructive of its spontaneous and instinctive self-unfolding. Yet this immediate loss prepares an eventual gain. False political and economic theories have led the way to truth, at the cost of much evil that instinct and common sense would have avoided. Bad theologies have checked the spontaneous growth of religions; but the theological attempt must fail and do harm, before it can succeed and do good.

IV

CHARACTER OF AN UNIVERSAL RELIGION

NOW by the science of mechanics we can create machines; but by a science of religion we could no more create a religion than we could create life by the science of biology. Yet what we cannot create, we can condition; and so far the science of religion may have immense practical value. There have been and may yet be new religious institutions; but there has not been and never can be a new religion, any more than a new language. Each is a bifurcation of some branch that is itself a bifurcation; and all can trace their origin to a common stem that has grown out of a root-idea—the idea of religion. However strange the new differentiating elements may be, yet they are united under categories inherited from the past and belong to the general process. We cannot, then, expect a new religion, but only a religion renovated and transformed by knowledge and understanding. And that renovation will be easiest for the system which has spontaneously and empirically realised most of the conditions of a true Catholicism. For others it will be more difficult or even quite impossible.

We have already rejected the notion of any sort of organic unity between the various forms of religion, as though they complemented one another, and constituted, when taken together, one full and connected expression of the religious idea. It is true that some are rich where others are poor; that we gain from all a fuller idea of religion than from any one, just as we gain a fuller idea of life from the whole animal kingdom than from man alone—microcosm though he be. Yet their unity is only logical. They are exclusive and hostile, rather than complementary. In each, religion strives to realise, not a part but the whole of her nature, within the given conditions of possibility. But in some few she succeeds far more amply; and these, in a limited sense, are her microcosms, embracing in a higher synthesis the advantages of many others, though not of all.

Now it is these microcosmic religions, which have already attained a certain relative catholicity, that are most capable of assimilating and profiting by the laws of religion, should these ever be established by historical and psychological science. It is easier to lop off excrescences and spurious developments than to take on characteristics that are real only when they have grown out of a remote past, and that may be excluded by the very constitution of the religion in question. Thus Lutheranism is a development, not of Catholicism from which it is a departure, but of certain elements of Catholicism; Liberal Protestantism is a development of certain elements of Lutheranism. At the first rending, when the wound was raw, the rejected elements might have been reassumed. But when the accepted elements were developed apart from the others and became a completed organism, rounded off and exclusive, no such restoration as this was possible. So, by their very formation and history, many religions exclude the possibility of Catholicity. They have cut off too much and cannot take it on again.

It seems to me, then, that true Catholicism is more likely to be realised in one of the older, wider, more chaotic, more spontaneous religions, than in any of those more plausible simplifications, which are shaped by a premature and somewhat *a priori* conception of what religion is and ought to be. Its chaos may contain more than is needed for the cosmos of law and order, but it is less likely to run short of the required elements.

Especially does this seem to be the case with Catholic Christianity, which is more nearly a microcosm of the world of religions than any other known form; where we find nearly every form of religious expression, from the lowest to the highest, pressed together and straining towards unification and coherence; where the ideal of universal and perpetual validity has ever been an explicit aim; where, moreover, this ideal is clothed in a form that cannot possibly endure the test of history and science and must undergo some transformation.

Now the reasons for this hope I have already given, in outline, in the opening chapters of *Through Scylla and Charybdis*, and it is not necessary to enlarge upon them here. Moreover, in the earlier part of this volume, I have given my reasons for believing that Catholicism is in substance, and to a large extent even in form, true to the idea of Jesus; that it develops the whole of that idea, and not merely certain elements of it. Catholicism preserves not only the ethical teaching of Jesus and His insistence on inwardness, but likewise His outwardness, His supernaturalism, His belief and hope in the other world, His sacramentalism and so forth. I do not say that all is development and that nothing is mere accretion or impurity; I say only that no essential element has been dropped. Other forms of religion have taken some of these elements and have developed them apart. This has not been without advantage for the elements in question which, in Catholicism, have had to wait on the growth of the whole idea to which they belong. It is easy to show that the sects have a better appreciation of this or that feature of Christianity than has the Church. But perhaps they have it at the cost of a false simplification and an impoverishment of the Christian idea.

I need only indicate here what seem to me to be quite objective and impersonal reasons for regarding Christianity as the highest spontaneous development of the religious Idea and, therefore, the religion most capable of reflective development, in the light of a science of religion gleaned from historical and psychological investigation, i.e. most capable of becoming as catholic and perpetual as that science.[1]

We have defined religion as being, practically, the adjustment of our conduct to a transcendent world. Such adjustment supposes that the transcendent is, in some way, revealed and felt as interfering with ordinary experience. The crooked tree, the oddly shaped stone, the thunderstorm, the earthquake, prior to any sort of reflection, created a feeling of wonder and fear, which suggested the thought of an unseen, incalculable and, possibly,

[1] In this I am following, with certain modifications, the line of thought suggested by Th. Steinmann's admirable work, *Die geistige Offenbarung Gottes in der geschichtlichen Person Jesu* (Vandenhoech and Ruprecht, Gottingen, 1903).

malign, power, to be appeased and propitiated. The first notions of the transcendent, its self-revelation and its propitiation, are materialistic, gross, entirely unethical and unspiritual. Man ignorantly worships the powers of nature, not a power above nature. If, at this stage, he also ignorantly worships the true God, it is in so far as he renders disinterested homage to the first whispers of his undeveloped conscience. His religion is but the servant of his temporal necessities; a means not an end. Such religions are formless and multitudinous.

Later, when he is civilised, we encounter tribal and state religions, whose gods are practically in the service of the collectivity. They sanction, with rewards and penalties, the customs and laws of the tribe, they go forth with its armies, they watch over all its temporal interests; all this in return for certain sacrifices and services. In the measure that the gods are exalted and that laws and customs are held to have been revealed by them and to be the expression of their will, religion begins to claim a certain independence and superiority over the people. They are God's people, if not actually His sons and descendants. They serve His will, rather than He theirs. If they offend Him He will cast them off. His attitude towards them is revealed in their prosperity or calamity. If things

s

go wrong, someone has sinned and must suffer. As laws and customs become less arbitrary, more just and reasonable, God's will is what is just and reasonable; He is a God of Righteousness. Ethics take over the paraphernalia of religion, which becomes a service of the righteous and true God by righteousness and truth.

At this stage religion sits in judgment on the state itself. We must obey God rather than men. But God is still an outside Power revealed in outside wonders, in rewards and chastisements, and served by external deeds and abstentions. He is the just Ruler and Judge of all the earth, but not yet a ruler of hearts and thoughts and desires. This comes with a further deepening of the moral sense; with the perception that inward principles and virtues are more important than those outward fruits, which can be imitated, that God searches the heart and the reins, that Goodness and Righteousness, in a word, are inward and not outward.

But even so God is an external, though heart-reading, Judge and reveals Himself by external interferences; by a miraculous book, by spoken oracles, by inspired teachers and law-givers. The principles of righteousness are imparted from without and accepted by faith in, and obedience to, an external teacher. The believer is in a state of tutelage, as an art student whose work is still imitative, and not creative or original; who is acquiring the spirit through obedience to the letter.

Through such an obedience, such an application of principles taken on trust, the spirit of art or of morality or of religion, which precedes all rules and principles as their source, is wakened to self-consciousness, and recognises its kinship with that spirit which is striving to express itself in the historical process of art, science, morality and religion. It recognises that the whole process is due to the same spirit, striving to realise itself in each individual through the medium of human society and tradition; striving to make the life of each man a divine and universal life, governed by a sympathy with the Divine Will and work in the whole process of history; in such sort that each shall become an instrument or organ of the Divine action, and take the whole world into himself as his own concern. Man is then no longer a servant or imitator of the Divine Will, but a son of God, a free and original co-operator in the Divine work. He is not the slave, but the master of the letter, which he respects so far as it is the utterance of the spirit by which he is governed. Now it is no longer from without, but from within, that God reveals Himself as a mysterious, transcendent force, counteracting and interfering with the natural order of events, overcoming the forces of egoism and individualism, and, through the action of spiritual personalities, interfering with the course of history as shaped by natural, self-centred man.

In the first stirrings of primitive conscience man is already solicited, as by an unknown God, to embrace the life of the spirit; to live for an universal and disinterested Good. At the end of the religious process he explicitly recognises this inward principle as the Divine Spirit, the condition and foundation of his personality. For what is personality if not that which is divine in man, that which makes him master of the determinism of nature of which he is at first the slave?—" Thou hast made him but little lower than God. Thou hast put all things under his feet." And to the fulness of this personality he can only attain by identifying himself with that indwelling Spirit which is transcendent over nature.

V

THE RELIGION AND PERSONALITY OF JESUS

THERE is a lower mysticism that is content to wrest the soul from the tyranny of the external by ascetical self-isolation, by forgetting the world and the historical process, in which the Divine Will reveals itself; that lives for rare moments of almost sensible contact with the indwelling Divinity. However narrowly indifferent to ethics, science and history, this mysticism emphasises one-sidedly the great truth that conscious union with God is the fullest realisation of humanity, the secret of that personality which sets man above nature. But it fails to recognise that this means union with a Will that is at work in the whole process of history and in every human soul. It is, as it were, a form without content.

Not such was the mysticism of Jesus that, in embracing God, embraced the whole world and all its spiritual interests—truth of feeling, truth of conduct, truth of knowledge; that forced Him into conflict with evil, reckless of reward or success, by the mere impetus, the imperative necessity of the

Divine Nature—"driven by the Spirit." "A new creature," a spirit, a personality, a Son of God—this is the full fruit of Christian Mysticism.

Jesus did not despise or turn away from the law of God, or the temple of God, in putting above both the Spirit that had created them and had revealed itself through them—as it were through sacraments and beggarly elements. At most He desired to supplement and fulfil the necessarily ever-imperfect expressions of the spirit; to push the letter down to its proper place of subordination and instrumentality; to carry religion to its final phase; to deny the static immutability and perpetuity of the external embodiment of the spirit, and to make it a living and growing organism.

When He opposes "But I say unto you," to "Moses said unto you," it is plain that He regards Himself as the Spirit incarnate, possessed of a human frame and soul, and uttering itself within all the natural limitations of local thought and language. It was through Him that Moses had spoken; what Moses *had*, He *was*. S. Paul is a true interpreter when he identifies Christ with the Spirit; when he speaks of the indwelling of the Spirit as the indwelling of Christ. So mastered and enslaved by the Spirit was Jesus, that His life was simply the life of the Spirit; His words the words of the Spirit. Against the Spirit

He had no freedom, but only within the limits of the Spirit. If He could not sin it was because the Spirit cannot sin.

In this sense we can deny Him a human personality. Man can progressively subject himself to the Spirit, but with the liberty of rebellion. He is not overmastered by it in spite of himself. But the personality, the "I," that speaks and acts in Jesus, is the Spirit, though it speaks and acts through the limitations of a human organism. It is the Spirit made man. The Word which enlightens every man is made flesh; what works within us stands before us, to be seen and heard and handled. In Him we have seen the Father—not in His fulness, but so far as God is inclusively the ideal image of man; so far as God reveals man to himself in a Divine Humanity. He comes, so to say, and lives our life Himself.

Thus it was that, for Christianity, Jesus and the Spirit became interchangeable terms; that the birth of the Spirit in man's soul became a birth and indwelling of Jesus. The inevitable anthropomorphism of man's conceptions of the Divine received a sanction:

> "So, through the thunder, comes a human voice,
> Saying: O heart I made, a Heart beats here."

"My little children," says Paul, "of whom I am again in travail until Christ be born in you"—all the instructions, precepts and exhortations of the Christian religion fall short of their purpose if they but make a man an obedient imitator of Christ, as it were of the first founder and example of a new religious system; if they do not evoke that Spirit which was incarnate in Jesus, and therefore *is* Jesus. Jesus was not merely a revealed ideal of human personality, but a forceful, living, self-communicating ideal; a fire spreading itself from soul to soul. It is only personality that works on personality. We can take precepts and instruction impersonally; we can obey and follow them and build them into the structure of our mental and moral habits. But we can sometimes apprehend the whole spirit and personality of a man through his words and acts and manner. We can feel him as an overwhelming personal influence; we can catch the concrete living spirit from the broken letters and words in which it utters itself. We can feel him living in us as a masterful force. We know his way and his will in a manner that no instruction could ever impart.

This it is that distinguishes Christianity from the following of a teacher or prophet. It teaches the precepts of Christ as a means to a birth of Christ in the soul—to the constitution of a divine personality within us; of a spirit that shall supersede all law and precept, as itself the source and the end of all law. Jesus Himself was the great sacrament and effectual symbol of the Divine Life and Spirit. He worked on His disciples, not doctrinally as a teacher of the understanding, but with all the force of a divine and mysterious personal ascendency, transmitted through every word and gesture. He was not a prophet speaking in the name of the Spirit, but the Spirit itself in human form. He spoke as only conscience can speak. Men heard and obeyed, they knew not why. He entered into their souls and possessed them and shaped them to His own image and likeness. When He left them externally, He was still with them internally. Conscience took shape and it was the shape of Jesus. Struck down by conscience Paul cries: "Who art thou, Lord?" and the revealing answer comes: "I am Jesus, whom thou persecutest." To this he refers when he says it was the good pleasure of God " to reveal His Son *in me;* I live, and yet no longer I, but Christ liveth *in me.*" In what other religion do men so speak of their founder, however loved and revered and followed? Personality is the end, and personality, mediated no doubt through external signs and symbols, is the means. Fire is kindled from fire. The Spirit of Jesus uttered in the Church, in the Gospel, in the sacraments, is apprehended by His followers, not as a doctrine but as a personal influence, fashioning the soul to its own divine nature.

It is impossible for spirit or personality to find adequate expression in terms of another order of experience. It is by a sort of internal sympathy that we read the personality of another out of the meagre shorthand of words and acts and gestures, and only so far as we are latently capable of realising a similar personality in ourselves. The vehicles and sacramental symbols, through which the Spirit communicates itself, are no part of the Spirit. The human frame and mind of Jesus, His local and temporal limitations of thought and knowledge, were but the sacramental elements through which the influence of His Divine Spirit was mediated. To our age He would have spoken differently, but the spirit would have been the same. A great artist, who makes the most of the poor materials and methods to hand, can reveal his spirit to a sympathetic apprehension as well as in a richer language; it is the spirit that quickens, the flesh profiteth nothing. The material imitation of the historical Christ tends to extinguish His Spirit. In us Christ, the Spirit, lives and utters Himself in the ever-changing forms of thought and language. In this sense S. Paul says that, if we have known Christ after the flesh, we shall know Him so no longer, but only after the spirit as the Heavenly Adam, the Son of Man, the Spirit of God. We have long since outgrown those apocalyptic forms of religious thought in which the Spirit of Jesus first uttered itself as the Son of Man—the Jewish Messiah. But the spirit itself we have not outgrown, and in us it seeks ever new forms wherein to clothe the same revelation.

This, then, is the special characteristic of Christianity. It does not look back upon Jesus, as a Franciscan might look back on S. Francis, or a Moslem on Mohammed, as being the founder of the society to which he belongs and the first example of that system of spirituality which has been handed down to him. It looks back on Jesus as being the Divine Spirit revealing itself in human form; as Himself the revelation of God; as communicating, not His ideas or His doctrines, but His very self, His spirit and personality to the soul, through the sacramental power of the Gospel and the Church; as constituting the salvation of the soul, its communion with God, its eternal life, by His personal indwelling. To be, as it were, "possessed" by Jesus is to be possessed by the Spirit of God. Those who lay hold of Him, who cluster round Him like swarming bees round their queen, become His very members, quickened by that Spirit which He was; they in Christ and

Christ in them, Christ in God and God in Christ, "that they may be perfected into One."

This is what we find from cover to cover of the New Testament. If it be more explicit in the Paulo-Johannine writings, it is fully implicit and partly explicit in the synoptic Gospels. This is what we find in the great Christo-Catholic tradition—" Christ in you, the hope of glory "—a quickening Spirit, an overwhelming personal influence, killing self and sin by a filial and self-sacrificing love of God, and of all the world as in God and from God and for God. This, too, is what we find in those Protestant bodies that, in breaking with the integrity of the Catholic tradition, have retained its central value, and for whom the name of Jesus is not merely that of a founder and teacher, but of a sacramental, self-communicating personality, to be laid hold of and appropriated; of One Who reveals Himself in each several soul as He did in the soul of S. Paul; of One through Whose intermediating humanity the soul is united to God.

This is what we do not find in that Liberal Christianity for which Jesus is to the Christian only what Mohammed is to the Moslem—the founder and teacher of a society, revealing and exemplifying a doctrine and method. Hence a philosophic chill, which increases in the measure that criticism puts Jesus back in His own century and surroundings, and forbids us to read into His human mind the ideas and presuppositions of our own day, or to see in Him a practicable example of what we now mean by life.

Those for whom He is a living indwelling spirit, a fire kindling from soul to soul down the long centuries, who see the expression of that spirit, not merely in the mortal life and thoughts of the Galilean carpenter, but in those of His followers who have been possessed by the spiritual and eternal personality of Jesus, have no such trouble in the face of criticism. It is no more to them that He was a first-century Jew in His mental outlook than that He was a man and a carpenter. What they live by is not His human mind but His divine spirit and personality, revealed in conflict with His human limitations and with ours, and with those of all generations to come. Had He spoken the language of the twentieth century, would He be intelligible to the fortieth, were it His language and not His personality that He had to communicate and reveal?

Is it any depreciation of the great military geniuses of the past to say that, if suddenly plunged into the midst of a modern engagement, they would be worse than worthless; that, without the requisite knowledge and experience, their genius would be useless? Yet do we not desiderate that same genius for our own leaders, without which all their knowledge and experience is of no avail? What are the categories and concepts of Jesus to us? Are we to frame our minds to that of a first-century Jewish carpenter, for whom more than half the world and nearly the whole of its history did not exist; to whom the stellar universe was unknown; who cared nothing for art or science or history or politics or nine-tenths of the interests of humanity, but solely for the Kingdom of God and His righteousness? And even in regard to this supreme interest is it His religious ideas, His apocalyptic imagery, that we are to take over, and not rather the spirit of which they were the inadequate embodiment—the best possible just for that time and place and no other? Would the military genius of the past tie us down to his weapons and methods of warfare? Would he not have desired and hoped that every generation should, while retaining his spirit, improve on his methods? And would not such improvements be the work of his own spirit?

To demand that Jesus should have had all the knowledge of Solomon is on a par with demanding that He should have had all the earthly riches and glory of Solomon. The note of the Gospel is that God has not chosen the great things of this world, but the small; not the rich, but the poor;

not the learned, but the simple. The elect of the world are not the elect of the Spirit; Solomon in all his glory was not arrayed as one of these. Why, if God did not disdain the rôle of a poor man and a tempted man, should He disdain that of an ignorant man, wherein to reveal the Spirit victorious over the very commonest human limitations? It is not from the human mind that He *had*, but from the Divine Spirit that He *was*, that man has drawn strength to conquer ignorance and weakness, energy to fight against darkness and wickedness, however costly, however interminable the conflict. To fill us with this Spirit was the mission of Jesus; not to teach us metaphysics or science or history or ethics or economics. The love of truth, the spirit of truthfulness, is the living root of all mental progress. This the most ignorant man may have and communicate.

This idea of Jesus as the Divine indwelling and saving Spirit seems to me the very essence of Christianity. Faith in Christ never meant merely faith in a teacher and his doctrine, but an apprehension of His personality as revealing itself within us.

There is no special difficulty in admitting that the dawn of a new epoch should be associated with the name of some individual who, however much the product of his time and sensitive to its spirit and needs, creates a new synthesis of all he has received, with some new and original contribution of his own. That, after all, is the law of spiritual development. Each spirit is evoked and shaped by the collective spirit of the day and shapes it in turn; as a rule imperceptibly, because in the straight line of its actual development.

But there come periods when a change of direction or of level is the condition of progress, and such new epochs are associated, whether in art, science, invention, politics or religion, with the name of some individual who, conscious of the *impasse*, discovers a way out and draws the whole world after him. It is no scandal to us that only those who come within the sphere of that man's influence enjoy the advantages thereof. But it seems intolerable that only those who have heard the name and the teaching of Jesus of Nazareth should attain eternal life; that two-thirds of present humanity, and nine-tenths or far more of past humanity, should fail of salvation.

Yet this would follow were the personality that spoke in Jesus that of a man, and not that of the Spirit which speaks to every man in the mysterious whisperings of conscience; were Jesus not simply the incarnation of conscience, the manifestation of that ideal humanity which conscience is striving to reveal to, and realise in, every human soul. So

He is interpreted in the Paulo-Johannine writings and in Catholic tradition. Because He did not merely possess, but *was* personally the true Light that enlightens every man, the indwelling Logos or Word of God, He could say: " I *am* the Way and the Truth and the Life, no one cometh unto the Father but by Me"; " He that hath the Son hath the life."

Hence all who are saved are saved through Christ, whose personality is that of the indwelling Spirit. Christianity has but brought the universal principle of salvation to its highest degree of force and explicitness. Conscience, that is first dimly felt as a mysterious influence interfering with and transcending the natural self and its laws, is revealed at last as the Spirit or Personality incarnate in Jesus.

VI

THE CHURCH AND ITS FUTURE

IF Christ be more than a teacher, the Church is more than a school; if He be more than a founder, the Church is more than an institution—though it is both one and the other. It is not merely related to Him as the Franciscan or Jesuit orders are to S. Francis and S. Ignatius, or the Wesleyans to John Wesley. This difference is well marked in the Pauline writings and belongs to the Catholic tradition. The Franciscan order is not the "mystical body" of S. Francis, however it seek to be imbued with his spirit, by way of imitation and by the following of its founder and teacher. It is only by a strained metaphor that S. Francis can be said to live in his true followers. The spirit that lives in them is that which was incarnate in Christ and which dwelt in S. Francis. S. Francis but taught his followers a way to Christ. His work was the work of a prophet.

But the Church of S. Paul is the mystical body of Christ—an extension of that human frame through which His spirit and personality communicated itself to His disciples, as it were sacramentally, i.e. in the way that a personality makes itself felt, as opposed to the way in which a teacher imparts a doctrine. In both cases signs are necessary; but in the latter thought speaks to thought, in the former spirit to spirit; in the latter an idea, in the former a force is transmitted. Through the mystical body, animated by the Spirit, we are brought into immediate contact with the ever present Christ. We hear Him in its Gospel, we touch and handle Him in its sacraments. He lives on in the Church, not metaphorically but actually. He finds a growing medium of self-utterance, ever complementing and correcting that of His mortal individuality. Thus it is through the instrumentality of the Church and its sacraments that His personality is renewed and strengthened in us; that the force of His spirit is transmitted and felt. The Church is not merely a society or school, but a mystery and sacrament; like the humanity of Christ of which it is an extension.

It is just this view of the Church that stands or falls with the Catholic conception of Jesus, as the name of the Divine Spirit acting the rôle of a man; and not merely as the name of a man, conforming himself to the inspirations of that spirit as to those of another personality. Where this belief has failed the Church is but a society of the disciples of a bygone prophet, a teacher who taught an age and a mentality that are almost entirely obsolete, whose personality and example grow less and less intelligible and illuminating as he recedes into a remoter past.

Explain it how we will, it is this conception of the spirit and personality of Jesus as an abiding presence in the Church; as coming in contact with the soul through her and her sacraments, above all in the mystery of the Holy Communion, which is explicitly the communication of His personality and eternal life—it is this conception that, for the Catholic Christian, makes the Church a sacrament rather than a society; a sacrament not invalidated by the meanness of the "beggarly elements" through which the Spirit is communicated.

Illusion though it be to some, it is a great thought, a stimulating belief, that breaks down the barriers of time and place; makes Jesus present to every soul, not only imaginatively but effectively; lends His human form and face and voice and name to "the Light which lighteth every man," to the Spirit that reveals itself in the first glimmerings of conscience. Take away this faith in Christ, and Catholicism ceases to be Christian, even though it still reverence Him as a founder, guide and example. Given this faith in Christ, and we have

Christianity even where the integral Catholic tradition is lacking: as in the uncritical Gospel-Christianity of so many of the sects.

As for so-called Liberal Protestantism, it is hard to see in what sense it can be called Christian. For in no sense was Jesus the originator of that conception of theistic righteousness which He adopted. He was at most an eminent disciple of the best rabbinical piety of His day. He brought it into His teaching and passed it on to His Church. If this doctrine of righteousness constitute the sole value to be sifted out of Catholicism, we have a system, not founded, but only transmitted, by Christ. It may be an excellent religion but it is not Christianity, either in its end or in its means. It could come to terms more easily with Islam than with Catholic Christianity, and belongs to the same stage of the religious Idea—to the prophetic stage.

But a religion to be truly Catholic, to be educative of all sorts and conditions of men and of every stage of man's religious progress, must represent every phase of the religious Idea, from the lowest to the highest, and not the highest alone. The process of the race repeats itself in the individual. Man does not begin, but ends by being spiritual and personal; first that which is earthly, afterwards that which is heavenly; milk for babes, meat for the strong. The law is but a pedagogue to lead us to Christ, though the fruit is implicit in the seed and Christ in the first whisperings of conscience. A Catholic religion will lead the soul through externalism to internalism. Ideally, the value of the lower is absorbed into and saved by the higher. Practically, in existing Catholicism, it is not so. We find these different sorts of religion ranged side by side, each subsisting with its own alloy—the religion of fear, the religion of hope; the religion of external and of internal obedience; the religion of abstract and exclusive mysticism, and that of inclusive and world-embracing mysticism. In his *Mystical Element of Religion* Baron F. Von Hügel has shown that, if the ideal synthesis of the institutional, rational and mystical elements be unattainable, owing to a sort of natural antipathy between them, yet the perpetual struggle after that ideal is essential; that the health of a religion consists in the balancing and holding together of principles that tend to fly asunder and become independent and exclusive.

So it is that, in existing Catholicism, the various phases of the religious Idea, each with its particular alloy and limitation, are somewhat violently held together by a continual synthetic effort, so as to constitute a manuductory system, by which the growing soul is brought to the perfect stature of the Christ-possessed personality. This has been the work of instinct and experience, rather than of design directed by a recognition of the laws of religion. It has all the imperfection and clumsiness of tentative gropings. But it gives us good reason to think that Catholic Christianity is more capable of conforming itself to the exigencies of a historical science of religion than any of those forms that have narrowed themselves to the development of some particular element of Catholicism, even though it be the highest. In fact, the science of religion would, in some sense, be a science of Catholicism; of a microcosm in which the whole religious process of the world is represented.

Modernists are not such utopian dreamers as to imagine that those, whose temporal interests are vested in existing Catholicism and its worst corruptions, will ever open their arms to welcome such a science. Which of the sciences have they not persecuted? Much more will they persecute that which deals with religion itself, their peculiar field of exploitation. The control of men's consciences, and, thereby, of their conduct and resources, is too valuable a weapon of aggrandisement not to be grasped at by the secular power, be it that of Czar or King or Republic; of papal monarchy or the bureaucracy that works for its restoration.

It is not of Catholicism in the grip of the exploiter, but of Catholicism as a living and lived religion, as a school of souls, that Modernists are thinking. Opposed tooth and nail by the exploiters of religion, science after science has made its way and found harbourage in the general mind, even of Catholicism—the most exploited because the most widely influential of all religions and the most dangerously independent in its principles. Hence the exploiter has ever striven to subject the consciences and personalities of its members to the divine right arrogated to himself.

What tyranny ever voted its own destruction or admitted a truth fatal to its interests? Will the Roman bureaucracy, that exploits even the Papacy, ever resign their revenues and their ascendency? Modernists do not believe it for a moment. Their whole hope is in the irresistible tide of truth and knowledge, which must at last surround and overmount the barriers of ignorance, buttressed up by untruthfulness; and, above all, in such inward and living Christianity as may still be left in a rapidly dying Church. Is it not the very growth of the spirit that is straining the old categories and forms and seeking a better embodiment—and this more especially in Catholicism, where the strain is most acutely felt and the pretensions of the exploiter are revealed by their growing shamelessness?

While such hopes, be they ever so delusive, live in him, why should the Modernist leave his Church? Where else will he find the true Catholicism of which he dreams? In this or that body he may find some neglected principle of Catholicism, emphasised and developed, but in isolation from the rest and at the cost of integral Christianity. He would find a religion as little, or less, Catholic in fact, and far less in potentiality.

An idealist is not necessarily a fool. He sees further, though more dimly, than the practical man, who calculates on inductions from the past, and on the presumption that no new factor will intervene. Yet what he sees may be true. The Modernist knows, not only as much of the difficulties of his ideal, but a great deal more than the Protestant or free-thinking critic, who sums him up in a smart article, whether encouraging or discouraging; and, accordingly, he is neither encouraged nor discouraged.

The reason why, fronted by the same data, one man hopes and another despairs, is just a difference of personality, temperament and experience. Hence even those who see eye to eye with the

Modernist may not, and in most cases will not, agree with him. But they will respect the hope which they do not share, while those who despise this hope cannot truly understand it.

It is the spirit of Christ that has again and again saved the Church from the hands of her worldly oppressors within and without; for where that spirit is, there is liberty. Deliverance comes from below, from those who are bound, not from those who bind. It is easy to quench a glimmering light caught by the eyes of a few; but not the light of the noonday sun—of knowledge that has become objective and valid for all. It is through knowledge of this kind that God has inaugurated a new epoch in man's intellectual life and extended his lordship over Nature. Shall He do less for man's spiritual life when the times are ripe? and are they not ripening? Are we not hastening to an *impasse*—to one of those extremities which are God's opportunities?